Storytelling across the Primary Curriculum

Starting from the question 'what is a story?', *Storytelling across the Primary Curriculum* leads the reader through the theory and practice of storytelling as an educational method – a method taught by the author over the past ten years through Primary English teaching programmes.

This practical book gives teachers the skills and confidence to use storytelling and the spoken word in the classroom in new and exciting ways. It will also help them to 'put down the book' and trust themselves to tell, rather than read, a story. It provides a wealth of examples of cross-curricular teaching opportunities, including a section on how the teaching of phonics can be embedded in the 'real' language of story.

Storytelling across the Primary Curriculum is ideal for trainee and practising primary school teachers who want to develop their classroom practice within the field of story-telling. Students on BA Primary, BEd and PGCE courses, particularly those specialising in English, will also benefit from this book's stimulating and intuitive approach to teaching English language and literacy.

Alastair K. Daniel has more than twenty years' experience in education as a teacher and storyteller. Having previously taught Primary English at Kingston University, he is now Senior Lecturer in Language and Literacy in Education at London Metropolitan University.

Storytelling across the Primary Curriculum

Alastair K. Daniel

Routledge
Taylor & Francis Group

LONDON AND NEW YORK

First published 2012
by Routledge
2 Park Square, Milton Park, Abingdon, Oxon OX14 4RN

Simultaneously published in the USA and Canada
by Routledge
711 Third Avenue, New York, NY 10017

Routledge is an imprint of the Taylor & Francis Group, an informa business

British Library Cataloguing in Publication Data
A catalogue record for this book is available from the British Library

Library of Congress Cataloging in Publication Data
Daniel, Alastair K.
  Storytelling across the primary curriculum / Alastair K Daniel. — 1st ed.
    p. cm.
  1. Storytelling. 2. Education, Primary. 3. Storytelling in education. I. Title.
  LB1042.D295 2011
  372.67'7—dc23   2011021986

ISBN: 978–0–415–59859–0 (hbk)
ISBN: 978–0–415–59860–6 (pbk)
ISBN: 978–0–203–15537–0 (ebk)

Typeset in Bembo
by Keystroke, Station Road, Codsall, Wolverhampton

MIX
Paper from
responsible sources
FSC
www.fsc.org   FSC® C004839

Printed and bound in Great Britain by
TJ International Ltd, Padstow, Cornwall

Contents

Acknowledgements

Figure 11.1 Henri Matisse (1869–1954): *L'Escargot* (1953) reproduced by permission. © Succession H. Matisse / DACS 2011, © Tate, London, 2011

Figure 11.5 W.F. Yeames (1835–1918): *And When Did You Last See Your Father?* (1878). Reproduced by courtesy of the National Museums Liverpool

Figure 12.4 The Storytelling Club, Ravenstone Primary School. Picture courtesy of Ty Van Brown and Matthew Friday (2010)

Figure 12.5 Illustration taken from *The Arrival* by Shaun Tan (2007) published by Lothian Children's Books (an imprint of Hachette Children's Books)

Thanks are also expressed both to colleagues from London Metropolitan and Kingston universities for their support and feedback, and to Diane Craven for advice on the use of faith stories, and to Harvey and Paul for reading over chapters and invaluable help with typesetting.

Classroom storytelling

Introduction: Storytelling as the social art of language

'Once upon a time . . .'

'Long ago, when the world was still young . . .'

'Once, in a week of two Wednesdays . . .'

The opening words may vary, but the invitation to a story is rarely ignored. If the tale is told well, between 'Once upon a time' and '. . . they lived happily ever after', the listener's eyes widen, the lips part and the body leans forward as the tale transports them to another time and another place.

This is a book about the potential of the story told to enhance the way that language is used in the primary classroom. The premise is simple: narrative is the natural way in which humans organise information, and storytelling is the most immediate (and fundamental) means by which that narrative is communicated. There is a renaissance in storytelling both in schools and in the wider community. The fact that all over the country there are people running training courses for business leaders and politicians to improve their storytelling abilities is a testimony to how seriously the effective communication of narrative is being taken. In schools, of course, story has always been an essential component of a full and rich education, many teachers have found ways to bring narrative to life in their practice, and there are schools where storytelling, by teachers and children, is celebrated. However, there are still many teachers for whom the value of spoken language seems to be as a precursor to the written word. Storytelling, when it does occur, is perhaps reserved for a dedicated 'story time', or is employed during those literacy activities that are aimed specifically at developing speaking and listening skills (such as *Talk for Writing*). For some teachers, the thought of putting down a book and simply narrating a story as part of their teaching can be too threatening to contemplate; as one teacher informed a student recently, 'We read to the children in this school, we don't tell them stories.' Such reluctance is hard to understand when the teacher quoted will, almost certainly, build much of her teaching on narrative frameworks, and frequently rely on oral transmission of information. Storytelling is part of what we, as teachers, do, and narrative simply provides the means of organising the content of the tales that we tell.

Jerome Bruner's writing on the centrality of narrative to human experience makes him a champion for the deployment of story. In an interview, he remarked:

> Why are we so intellectually dismissive towards narrative? Why are we inclined to treat it as rather a trashy, if entertaining, way of thinking about and talking about what we do with our minds? Storytelling performs the dual cultural functions of making the strange familiar and ourselves private and distinctive.
>
> (Crace, 2007)

His phrase 'making the strange familiar' places story at the heart of all teaching, rather than belonging only to those times dedicated to the study of English as a subject area. As the most immediate means of communicating narrative (compared with printed text, acted script or danced choreography), storytelling represents a fundamental act of human exchange. From contextualising the teaching of systematic synthetic phonics in early reading to narrating the events of the Battle of Hastings; from explaining the planetary movement of the solar system to leading a whole-school assembly, storytelling provides a teaching strategy that works within the frameworks that humans naturally create for themselves as they organise information.

The centrality of story

In *The God Delusion* (2006), Richard Dawkins suggests that human beings will naturally look not only for reasons, but also for intentionality to explain events in the world around them. Citing the example of John Cleese's comic creation Basil Fawlty, Dawkins explains that people need to feel that the things that happen to them can be explained by reference to the intentional intervention of forces that stand outside themselves. When his elderly car fails him on an essential journey, Basil Fawlty pulls a branch from a tree and thrashes the vehicle and berates it: he punishes the car because it has intentionally let him down. However, Dawkins's scope is far larger than this trivial example. He suggests that, when faced with disasters such as earthquakes, humans look for reasons that go beyond the shift of tectonic plates, and that include an element of agency. From offended spirits to alien intervention, we look for someone to blame for events that lack a personified and intentional instigator. Whatever Dawkins's theorising suggests about the existence, or otherwise, of God, the notion of the human need to seek intentionality does suggest that humans are natural storytellers. Religious myths enshrine the ultimate causes of the fabric of the world, the nature of humankind, the relationships between people, the finality (or otherwise) of death and, of course, love. Fables, parables and folk tales link the folly of human behaviour to its consequences (whether losing the flock of sheep to the wolf, or the elevation of religious purity over the plight of the injured Samaritan). We appear to be programmed to ascribe intention and agency from early childhood. Bruner (1986) cites research in which people's reactions to a film of randomly moving objects were recorded. Adult subjects attributed intentionality to, and relationships between, objects as they moved together, and while this may not be startling, it was then found that six-month-old babies mirrored the reactions of the adults. With this basic 'programming' for how to read the world around us, we fill in gaps when information is incomplete, and create stories. While we may think that we know what makes us and our neighbours 'tick', in the absence of immediate knowledge, we use our imagination to attribute intention: animals are anthropomorphised so that we can recognise ourselves and others within them; nature assumes character and rewards or punishes (to devastating effect). In other words, humans are perpetually engaged in an imaginative exercise to explain the world around them — it is in this world of imagined causes that a car will decide for itself whether or not it will deliver a frustrated hotel owner to his Torquay destination.

In addition to looking for, and imaginatively creating, the causes and agents of events, humans categorise and sequence them. The experiences that fill our lives are ordered through the past and into the present and, based on these experiences, possibilities are projected into the future. It is in narrative that these events are organised and given meaning, thus we can see narrative as 'the principal way in which our species organizes its understanding of time' (Porter Abbott, 2002: 3).

Narrative, and its expression as story, may therefore be seen as central to our own understanding of what it is to live our lives in Barbara Hardy's famous phrase, 'a primary act of mind' (1978). This representation of our world is not simply an internal process, but is essentially social. In *Storytelling: Process and Practice* (1986), Norma Livo and Sandra Rietz provide a powerful rationale for seeing story as fundamental to the way in which human beings represent themselves to themselves and to each other:

> 'Story' is its own reality. It is a configuration in memory that is quite independent of the specific details of any given event. We all recognize 'story' and are easily able to distinguish between something told that is 'stories' and something that is not. 'Story' is a way of knowing and remembering information — a shape or pattern into which information can be arranged. It serves a very basic purpose; it restructures experiences for the purpose of 'saving' them and it is an ancient, perhaps natural order of mind — primordial, having grown along with the development of human memory and of language itself. 'Story' is a way of organizing language.
>
> (Livo and Rietz, 1986: 5)

This capacity to shape meaning through the language of story is a quality that has received increasing attention in education. In 2001, curriculum guidance on 'Storytelling aspects of narrative' was provided to English schools, which stated that narrative:

> is central to learning . . . It helps children to understand themselves and their world, giving shape and meaning to their experiences, organising their ideas, and structuring their thinking and, ultimately, their writing. Different cultures and communities make different use of stories, but storytelling and thinking through story remain universal human competences.
>
> (Storytelling aspects of narrative 2001)[1]

The writers have recognised not only the imaginative capacity of humans, but also their need to organise and, crucially, express their ideas and experiences (although writing is still regarded as the apogee of children's activity). It seems reasonable, therefore, to assert that when creating opportunities for children to learn, we should engage with narrative form and develop both our own competence with the language of story and that of the children we teach.

From narrative to story to storytelling

Before discussing the qualities that are particular to storytelling as a form of narrative expression (as opposed to story reading or story writing), these fundamental terms, 'story' and 'narrative', need to be clarified and differentiated.

In his meta-analysis of research into the use and effects of story and storytelling, Kendal Haven defines story as 'a detailed, character-based narration of a character's struggles to overcome obstacles and reach an important goal' (2007: 79). Story is descriptive and expressive; it creates mental images of characters, their struggles and their journey towards their goal. By contrast, the term 'narrative' is more functional, and is used in this book to refer to the underlying structure around which story is built. Narrative deals not with the descriptive and expressive elements of story, but with the way in which ideas are combined (later on, this distinction will help us apply storytelling techniques across the curriculum).

Of course, 'storytelling' is itself an ambiguous term. One may speak of storytelling and describe the works of novelists, playwrights and actors, and by utilising the word, these arts are located in an ageless tradition. However, such a catch-all description dilutes the meaning of 'storytelling', so that it comes to refer to any activity in which a story is created or communicated. In the classroom context, this has meant that storytelling has often been conflated with story reading and story writing, so that children are never given opportunities to engage in oral recounting of their own narratives (at least not without a prepared script), and the default activity is one in which words are committed to paper rather than given voice.

It is 'telling', then, that is the key: storytelling is not story writing, nor is it story reading. The storyteller has no written text from which to draw the words they use (although they may have started the preparation process with a written text); rather, they weave their language around a narrative framework to create a story for a particular group of people, at a particular moment, in a particular place. This means that the teacher/storyteller is thrown upon their own imaginative and linguistic resources in order to create the told story.

Storytelling and performance

The anxieties that some people experience at the thought of telling a story without notes or a prepared script (either on paper or memorised) were brought home to me when a student teacher commented, 'If I'd wanted to do this [storytelling] I'd have chosen drama, not English!' Coming from a second-year student preparing for an assessment of her ability to tell a story with a group of children in the presence of her peers and two examiners, perhaps the outburst was understandable. At this early stage in her developing understanding of the nature of classroom storytelling, this student saw storytelling as a performance akin to a one-woman show. The shift from a position of fear to one of confidence lies in the description of the assessment task: to tell a story 'with', not tell a story 'to'. Classroom storytelling is not about an 'I am' mode of performance (I am the actor, the character, the entertainer), but rather a collaborative, 'we are', mode, where storytelling becomes a social performance in which all members of the group (storyteller/teacher and children) make the story together.

It is possible, then, to reframe the 'p' word so that the positive and necessary elements of performance in storytelling can be emphasised, and the more unhelpful associations with theatre placed in the proper context.

The theatre anthropologist Richard Schechner refers to performance as 'twice performed' or 'restored' behaviour:

> Restored behaviour is living behaviour treated as a film director treats a strip of film. These strips of behaviour can be rearranged or reconstructed; they are independent of the causal systems (social, psychological, technological) that brought them into existence . . .

> Performance means: never for the first time. It means: for the second to the nth time. Performance is 'twice-behaved behaviour.'

> (Schechner, 1985: 35, 36)

Schechner explains that the term 'performance' covers behaviour that has been pre-prepared, even if not in the sense of the theatrical rehearsal. For Schechner, then, performance is about the construction of intentional behaviours. An alternative approach is taken by Erwin Goffman in his seminal work on social role, *The Presentation of Self in Everyday Life* (1959), in which he defines performance as behaviour that is directed by one party at achieving a change in a second party. Between these two definitions, we can see how this contentious word 'performance' can cover not only the actor portraying Ophelia (moving the emotions of a West End audience by the way she manipulates Shakespeare's text), but also the Year 4 teacher (working to a prepared lesson plan, leading their charges to a sounder understanding of long multiplication). In both instances, the 'performer' needs an ability to construct the content through meaningful combinations of different elements in order to bring about a change in their 'audience'. If we accept performance as behaviour that fulfils both Schechner's and Goffman's conditions, then classroom storytelling clearly falls within this description.

Part 1 of this book is divided into chapters that address the two faces of performance: behaviour that is both deliberately prepared, and aimed at achieving a change in those who experience it. Narrative is the organisational framework on which the 'restored behaviour' of storytelling is built, and so Chapters 2–4 consider the structure of narrative, the criteria for the selection of appropriate narratives, and the forming of narrative into tales that can be owned by the storyteller and shared by the learning community. In Chapter 5, the skills necessary for effective narrative communication are explored, including voice, non-verbal communication and controlling the storytelling environment. By using crafted language (on all its levels) to creatively communicate structured accounts, teachers can deepen children's experience of learning across the curriculum

Developing the storytelling community

This book is concerned primarily with the role of storytelling in the pedagogic process; in other words, the place of narrative in teaching and the role of the teacher as a storyteller. However, this role is to be shared: the performance of the teacher is one that includes the active participation of the children. Vivian Gussin Paley describes story as 'a shared process, a primary cultural institution, *the social art of language*' (1990: 23), and this model of a shared process is one that underpins my own understanding of story and the role of the storyteller in the classroom. With story as a social construction rather than a solo performance, the teacher becomes the principal storyteller in a classroom community of storytellers, and the competencies necessary to engage successfully in storytelling therefore need to be distributed.

Sharing the storytelling competence – allowing children to become critics, sages and seers

The term *competence* in the context of performance is borrowed from sociology: to have a competency means having the necessary skills to complete a task, and a context within which those skills can be successfully employed. For the actor playing Ophelia, her competency lies in her ability not only to learn the lines, but also to express them through voice and action in a way that is consistent with the character. However, although she may be able to deliver her lines as the character of Ophelia with great expression, the actor's ability to portray the character of Ophelia is also dependent on her fellow actors treating her as Ophelia and the audience's recognition of her in rôle as the person of Ophelia. In other words, even the high-end performance of classical theatre is dependent on more than the abilities of the actors – on a shared communal response to the performance event. In the classroom community of storytellers, a sense of communal competence lies at the core of the storytelling.

The idea of memorising a story by learning its structure rather than a script can be daunting for some people. However, avoiding language that is fixed, and developing the necessary skills to be flexible in retelling narrative, are vital skills in dispersing competence. If a teacher repeats a story word for word, action by action, without reference to the children with whom the tale is shared, the balance of competence lies squarely with the teller and their ability to perform a text. In such cases, the children's competence is restricted to the ability to listen – or (worse) to manifest those behaviours associated with listening. In a classroom community of storytellers, by contrast, the storytelling is characterised by a more even spread of the necessary competencies. The teacher/storyteller still needs a commitment to communicating the narrative ideas, but the storytelling becomes dependent on the children's contributions to such a degree that the telling could not happen without their interventions. The story, then, becomes particular to that group of children, in that context, and at that time.

A consequence of such an approach is, of course, that one of the necessary competencies of the storytelling teacher is the ability to listen to the children and be sensitive to their reactions. In Chapter 5 we explore some of the ways in which children and their ideas can be incorporated into the retelling of a narrative led by a teacher/storyteller. By creating space in which the children are able to comment on the narrative, predict outcomes, make suggestions to augment the story and offer critique, the competency to succeed in a particular piece of storytelling is shared. At the same time, as seers, children predict the trajectory of the narrative, identify problems likely to confront the characters and discuss possible solutions. In commenting on and critiquing stories, pupils not only step outside the imagined world to judge its internal coherence, but also respond to the devices used to communicate the narrative (which will include the non-verbal as well as the linguistic). This notion of story as a locus for summary, critique, prediction and projection is essential to the core message of communal storytelling.

Children as storytellers

The first part of this chapter proposed that story is the principal means through which human beings represent the world to each other. Because of this fundamental quality of narrative, we can argue that storytelling is an essential tool in every teacher's pedagogy. However, just as the ability to pattern oral language in story form is important for teachers, the development of the same abilities is equally important for children. Children's storytelling skills need to be both acknowledged and honed as part of their education.

English within the National Curriculum for England (DfEE, 1999) included the telling of story as an activity for Key Stage 1 within Speaking and Listening; this was explicitly extended into Key Stage 2 within the *Primary Framework for Literacy* (DCSF, 2007). There was, therefore, within the curriculum, an expectation that children should engage in storytelling for its own sake. The *Talk for Writing* materials which were produced by the National Strategies in cooperation with Pie Corbett (DCSF, 2008a) further raised awareness of the potential of children's storytelling to support their writing (this is explored in Chapter 6 of this book). At the time of writing, we are waiting for the details of the new National Curriculum for England but, whatever the outcome, many teachers have already rediscovered the value of children's talk, and it can be hoped that storytelling will continue to gain ground as a purposeful opportunity for children to engage in meaningful and sustained talk.

Moving beyond the language of story, storytelling demands skills that assist learning across the curriculum and on many levels. Opportunities for children to tell stories develop their abilities to sequence, present perspectives on a series of events, link effect to cause, and make choices that reflect a moral standpoint. In addition, children's social and emotional learning is supported by those aspects of telling associated with performance: expression, verbal and non-verbal fluency, understanding of pace and rhythm, social engagement with hearers, and memory.

The National Oracy Project's *Common Bonds: Storytelling in the Classroom* suggests ways in which storytelling can be used by children within the classroom – it can be used to:

- Allow pupils to learn and to demonstrate what they have learnt in a way that is revealing and motivating;
- Give an opportunity for information, events, thoughts and feelings to be explored, shaped, organised and expressed;
- As a way of explaining their understanding of a process, such as the functioning of the human digestive system;
- As an outcome of work on a topic, creating a collaborative story which is designed to reveal their understanding of, for example, the causes of pollution, or of an historical incident;
- As a way of exploring the various myths associated with creation in different cultures;
- As part of building with construction toys;
- As part of role play in the hospital corner, cafe, travel agent, or in other thematic areas set up by the teacher.

(Howe and Johnson, 1992: 8–9)

This list echoes the way in which storytelling has been applied to teaching across the curriculum in this book, but it also places storytelling at the heart of children's lives in the way they recount events and make sense of the world around them. Livo and Rietz's (1986) assertion that story is 'a way of organizing language' has as many implications for the need to provide opportunities for children to explore that story as a form of language, as it has for the way in which teachers present curriculum. Reflecting on her experiences with kindergarten children, Vivian Gussin Paley comments that children 'do not pretend to be storytellers; they *are* storytellers. It is their intuitive approach to all occasions. It is the way they think' (1990: 17).

The readiness of children to tell stories is evidenced in every classroom and every playground, not only during times of structured and pedagogic talk, but also between those moments, when the anecdote, joke and imagined world assert themselves. Planned opportunities for storytelling can allow children to use purposeful, sustained and creative language that can extend curriculum content or be an adjunct to it. The Storytelling Club at Ravenstone School in south London is an after-school club for Year 3 and Year 4 children, run by two young teachers, and one cannot help but be struck by the children's desire to participate and craft language (see Chapter 12). Active listening skills are brought to bear on an hour of activities as children create group stories, tell their own tales and act out each other's stories (as well as those of their teachers).

In the following chapters, there are suggestions for incorporating storytelling across the curriculum. Although some of these are aimed at the teacher as storyteller, and some at children as storytellers, all are intended as social events in which stories are created by all those present. It is here that I sense I have put myself on a collision course with the approach outlined in the National Strategies' *Talk for Writing* materials, based on work by Pie Corbett, which advocate a sequence of 'imitation – innovation – invention' (DCSF, 2008a: 7). The idea that children should learn a story through copying the teacher (who has learned the story from a script or recording) seems to work against the social nature of storytelling, where the telling is rooted not only in the person of the teller, but also in the community with whom they are sharing their story (which could simply be a talk-partner). I would suggest that there is a profound difference between the repetition of memorised phrases, and activities that provide a scaffold on which the language of story can be constructed. Corbett is clear that people should not learn stories word-for-word, and his developmental route of storytelling skills does coincide with the route from lower- to higher-order thinking skills: 'remember – understand – apply – analyze – evaluate – create' (Bloom, revised by Anderson and Krathwohl, 2001) but, I would suggest, it does not focus adequately on the highest level of thinking (creating). The emphasis on recalling a third party's version of a story fails to privilege the important aspects of analysis and evaluation used to understand story grammar, and the application of that analysis in the creation of owned narratives. The way that people recall stories is to structure the relationships within them, and then narrate the ways in which those relationships are affected by (and affect) events – when children are developing their storytelling skills, we should try to work with the way in which they naturally recount events, and avoid making storytelling dependent on what can easily become mechanistic repetition.

Having said all of the above, it is clear that one of the most important aspects of enabling children to be effective storytellers is ensuring that they have a developed story vocabulary. This is achieved through being exposed to a wide range of stories, and learning within a rich language context. Of course, the vocabulary of the told story is not simply linguistic, but depends on para-linguistic elements such as tone of voice, gesture and pace. Consequently, teachers cannot restrict children's stories to printed versions of stories, but provide experiences of oral retelling. In other words, teachers need to model the expressive potential of storytelling and foster the active community of storytellers.

Summary

In this introductory chapter, we have established the centrality of narrative to the organisation of human experience. By providing children with learning experiences constructed around story, we are giving them opportunities to learn within a framework that coincides with the way they structure thought. As an expression of narrative (without an intervening written text), the story told is the most immediate and personal medium of conveying experience and information. The story becomes the means by which teacher and child share perspectives on the events and ideas that are recounted. This creation of shared meaning is at the core of the approach outlined in this book: stories should be seen as negotiable expressions of narrative, rather than fixed language. They should be expressed in language that is adapted to the social context of their telling, and reflect their nature as what Vivian Gussin Paley calls the 'social art of language' (1990).

2

Building the framework: Narrative structure and meta-narrative

One of the principal aims of storytelling with children is to develop both their narrative awareness and their narrative thinking. In order to do this, the teacher needs to have their own sense of narrative structure. So, before going on to looking at story selection and adaptation, we will first establish a common language of narrative.

Story structure – developing common language

The simplest of narrative structures, familiar to children in Key Stage 1, is found in Aristotle's *Poetics*:

beginning – middle – end

This format perhaps seems simplistic, but its importance has to be understood in terms of narrative coherence: the relationship between these sections needs to be secure and lead from one to the other. Despite its common application in the West, this linear model is not, however, universal, and other world cultures have devised alternative approaches to narrative. In Figure 2.1, the Aristotelian beginning–middle–end model is compared with that of the Navajo people of North America and a common middle-eastern form in which stories are layered, one within another. In the Navajo tradition, stories are inextricably bound to the land and are cyclical in nature – their tales begin in the east, and then events follow in the south and west, with a resolution taking place in the north before the final return to the east. The middle-eastern example is taken from a collection of stories known as either 'Tales from the Arabian Nights' or 'Tales from 1001 Nights', and shows the story of 'The Sage Duban' embedded within the story of the 'Fisherman and the demon'. The latter tale tells of a poor fisherman who, rescuing a demon from his bottle-prison, is rewarded by a promise of death. The fisherman is surprised at the demon's ingratitude and wonders if the genie knows the story of the Sage Duban. When the demon confesses his ignorance, the fisherman tells

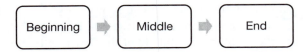

The Aristotelian linear model of narrative

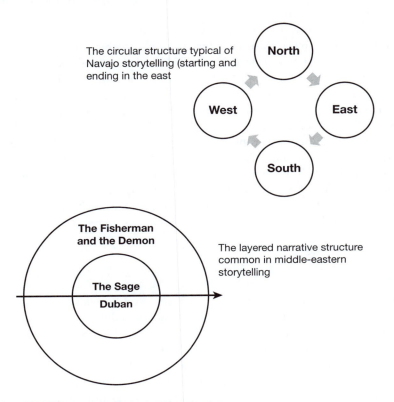

The circular structure typical of Navajo storytelling (starting and ending in the east

North

West

East

South

The Fisherman and the Demon

The Sage

Duban

The layered narrative structure common in middle-eastern storytelling

FIGURE 2.1 Variations on narrative structure

him the story of the wise man who takes his revenge on the king who has ordered his execution despite the Sage's curing him of leprosy. The second story's only relationship to the surrounding tale is the thematic content of ingratitude; it establishes a completely fresh list of characters, locations and situations.

For the purposes of this book we will remain, however, with the linear structure. Moving on to the next stage of complexity, we need to recognise the place of conflict in the structure, for without the presence of conflict, there is no real story. Conflict can be between individuals or groups, or an internal struggle, but this complication enables the narrative to become a quest towards solving the problem. At the end of the story, of course, the problem needs to be resolved and so the structure, which is now fivefold, looks like this:

beginning/introduction – problem – events/middle – resolution – end

A problem near the beginning of the story gives it a trajectory towards the resolution – a resolution does not necessarily mean that the problem is solved, nor that the quest is successful, but the events in the middle of the structure lead to the point where the problem either is overwhelmed, or overwhelms. By Key Stage 2, children should have moved on from the simple beginning–middle–end model, and be thinking of narrative in these, more complex, terms.

For the teacher/storyteller, this model provides a flexible framework that can be used to analyse the structure of linear narratives, reconstruct them, and then model the approach for children. However, we can add an additional layer of complexity that helps drive the story's trajectory and provide tension: climax or crisis. By placing a climactic event prior to the resolution of the problem, there is a sense of growing tension and then release. It is common to present this rise in tension as a mountain range, where smaller crises are reached at each successive and rising peak until the climactic event occurs on the topmost peak; from the highest peak, the 'falling action' then leads down to the resolution and ending. These representations are based on a model devised in 1863 by Gustav Freytag, which has been hugely influential in both the analysis of narrative and the world of script writing (his pyramid is shown in Figure 2.2). However, for ease of representation we will configure our model (introduction – problem – events leading to a crisis – resolution – end) as simple storyboards (see Figure 2.3).

Meta-narrative

When it comes to story memorisation, a linear approach can be can be invaluable in creating a storyboard. However, in order not only to judge whether a story (or account or process) is readily adaptable, but also to organise the essential elements of that story to create a new, owned and coherent narrative, linearity is not enough. The coherence of a narrative is not dependent simply on the way in which its elements are linked together from beginning to end, but rather on the relationships that exist between those elements. There have been many attempts to map these relationships by devising a grammar of story that could be applied across all narrative genres (from 'high' litera-ture to conversational anecdote). Possibly the most influential of these analyses (because of its groundbreaking nature) was Vladmir Propp's (1928) examination of Russian folk tales, *Morphology of the Folktale*, in which he listed thirty-one narrative *functions* (such

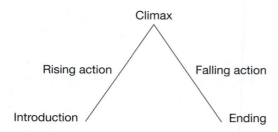

FIGURE 2.2 Freytag's pyramidal narrative structure

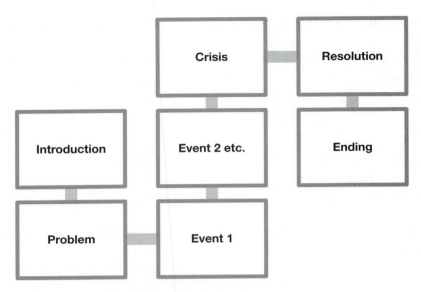

FIGURE 2.3 Linear narrative structure – storyboard

as villainy or departure) through which events developed. In addition, he suggested that there are eight *types* of which every character in Russian folklore is a variation (villain, donor, helper, princess or prize, father, dispatcher, hero, false hero). The revolutionary aspect of the analysis was that it didn't follow the narrative in a line from beginning to end, but instead identified the most influential elements of the narrative and analysed the relationships between these elements (Fox, 1993).

Coming out of Propp's work is an analytical tool, the 'actantial narrative schema', developed by the Czech émigré A.J. Greimas (Greimas and Courtes, 1979; Schleifer, 1987). Rather than listing the actions of the various characters in a story, Greimas looked at the way in which forces come to bear on the main characters and shape the events of the narrative. He suggested that at the heart of every tale there are six 'actantial functions', which may be filled by other characters, inanimate objects, forces or attributes. Postgraduate students have been known to go cross-eyed when first faced with this form of analysis but, once initial reluctance to dismember story in this forensic way is overcome, the reward is in being able to deconstruct and reconstruct simple narratives quickly. Greimas's schematic method has been an essential part of my own storytelling methodology for over ten years and, once grasped, it provides a simple and invaluable tool for manipulating narrative ideas in the classroom. The actantial narrative schema has a central place in the method outlined in this book.

The actantial functions are as follows:

- **subject**: the character around whom the narrative turns;
- **object**: that which the subject wants to achieve or acquire (this could be a person, an object or an attribute);
- **sender**: the person(s) or force(s) that moves the subject to seek the object;

- **receiver**: the person(s) that benefits from the subject's successful quest for the object;
- **helper**: the person(s) or force(s) that aid the subject in their quest for the object;
- **opponent**: the person(s) or force(s) that oppose the subject's completion of their quest for the object.

These form binary pairs:

- **subject** and **object**;
- **sender** and **receiver**;
- **helper** and **opponent**.

The pairs are usually arranged in diagrammatic form to create a narrative schema as shown in Figure 2.4.

In showing how the various functions act upon one another, the actantial schema is clearly not a linear representation of narrative. However, it is possible to render the analysis in a verbal form, which can be used with children at Key Stages 1 and 2. The functions can be identified through a series of simple questions:

- **subject**: who is this story about?
- **object**: what do they want to do?
- **sender**: what makes them want to do this?
- **receiver**: who will be happy if they do this?
- **opponent**: who or what is trying to stop them from doing this?
- **helper**: who or what is helping them to do this?

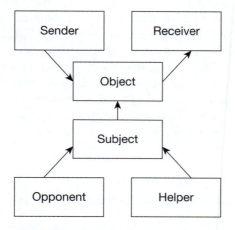

FIGURE 2.4 The actantial narrative schema (after A.J. Greimas)

If these questions are compared with the 'who, what, where, when' sequence, there are clear differences. The setting (spatial and temporal) of the story is not included in this analysis and needs to be considered in addition to the actantial analysis, but the analysis does extend the 'who' and 'what' questions with 'why' (the sender and receiver create the motivational force behind the narrative) and 'how' (the tension between the helper and opponent determine the means by which the subject tries to achieve their object).

An actantial analysis of the Brothers Grimms' version of 'Little Red Riding Hood'[1] is shown in Figure 2.5.

Having established the setting of the forest and 'a long time ago', we consider the six questions:

- **subject**: who is this story about?
  Little Red Riding Hood – a girl who lives with her mother and father;
- **object**: what does Little Red Riding Hood want to do?
  to take a basket of provisions to her grandmother in the forest;

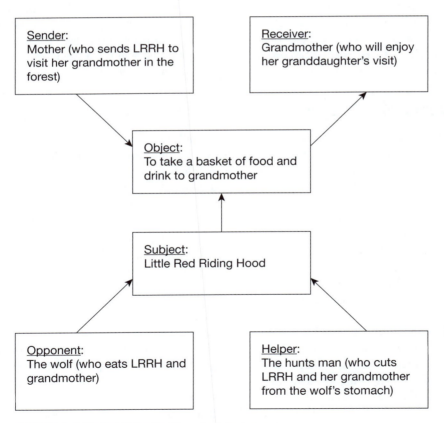

FIGURE 2.5 'Little Red Riding Hood' – actantial schema

- **sender**: what makes her want to do this?
  her mother is concerned because her grandmother is sick;

- **receiver**: who will be happy if she does this?
  her grandmother;

- **opponent**: who or what is trying to stop them from doing this?
  a wolf;

- **helper**: who is going to help her?
  a huntsman.

If we are unable to identify the six functions (which may be implicit rather than articulated), then the narrative will lack coherence. Without the sender or receiver, we have no idea why the events of the story unfold: without her mother's concern that her grandmother needs food and drink because she is ill, we have no idea why Little Red Riding Hood enters what is, after all, a dangerous forest. Without the opponent (in the shape of the wolf), grandmother receives her provisions and there is no drama; with no helper (the huntsman), the wolf's digestive juices are left to do their worst on both the little girl and her grandmother.

As stated at the beginning of this chapter, the question of suitability is one concerned with potential. Hence, if a story has fulfilled the primary criterion of being a 'tale waiting to be told', but lacks one or two identifiable actantial functions, the question is whether they can be created by the storyteller in the adaptation in a way that does service to the original and maintains thematic integrity.[2]

Structural elements of performance

The linear and meta-analysis of narrative outlined above can be applied to stories told or stories read. However, there are differences to be drawn between the story as it appears in printed text, and stories as they are told between people. Here we will draw on the work of William Labov, who analysed the conversations of young people in New York in the 1960s (Labov, 1972). His analysis is notable because, starting with a structure similar to our fivefold pattern, he identified additional elements that mark out the story told.

Prior to the introduction (*orientation* in Labov's terms), people about to tell a story normally provide an abstract – a short summary of what it to come. In conversation, this could be as simple as 'you won't believe what happened to me when I tried to use the photocopier' – an abstract that establishes something of the context and hints at crises to come. In more formal storytelling, the abstract could be, 'Here is a story about a princess whose long hair helps her find love.'

Following the story's resolution (and ending, in our model), the storyteller returns their listeners from the imagined world to the present time and space. In conversation, the story may conclude with a transitional statement that passes the narrative baton on to the next person: 'But enough about me and the photocopier, what about your day?' In more formal settings, storytellers have a variety of ways of ending a story – such as the responsorial refrain 'crick-crack' from the Caribbean tradition.

While the abstract and coda are important elements in ensuring that storytelling follows the pattern of natural conversational encounters, Labov's most significant contribution to understanding story structure is the notion of *evaluation*. In Labov's words, evaluation is:

> the means used by the narrator to indicate the point of the narrative, its *raison d'être*: why it was told and what the narrator is getting at.
>
> (Labov, 1972 in Toolan, 1988: 152)

The narrator is not a neutral observer of events, but a partisan commentator who makes value judgements about which characters we should empathise with and which we should condemn; which behaviour we should emulate and which we should avoid. These value judgements are achieved through asides and the way in which elements of the narrative are emphasised by choice of language, repetition, voice and body language. Carol Fox reflects that this analysis represented a breakthrough in narrative analysis:

> The crucial difference between Labov's analysis and others . . . Is that here at last great importance is attached to storytelling *style*, style which is not seen as unnecessary elaboration but rather the lifeblood of the story. . . Applying this model of structure . . . places affective aspects of story at the centre of the discourse
>
> (Fox, 1993: 75–76)

There are published versions of Labov's narrative structure that place the evaluation as a discrete section within the central (events) section of the narrative. However, Labov is clear that, although evaluative activity may be concentrated around the crisis and before the resolution, it can be spread throughout the storytelling.

Summary

This short chapter has outlined the three complementary ways of viewing narrative that will inform our approach to storytelling across the curriculum.

- The **linear narrative** (incorporating Labov's abstract and coda), which tracks the sequence of events that make up the story:
  (abstract –) introduction – problem – events leading to crisis – resolution – ending (– coda).
- The **meta–narrative**, which tracks the relationships between the different characters and forces within the story, and the way they impact on the protagonist: subject, object, sender, receiver, opponent, helper.
- The **evaluation** of the narrative, which can occur throughout the story (although it tends to be concentrated around the crisis) and expresses the storyteller's view of characters and events.

Storytellers have told their tales for millennia without any such analysis, and we, as *Homo narrans* – the storytelling animal (Foerst, 2005) – have no need of it in every retelling of our lives. However, these analytical tools serve to distil the approaches to narrative taken by storytellers throughout the world, and enable us to develop an awareness of the narratives that we adapt and share. In addition, as stated above, we, as teachers, need to have a secure narrative framework within which we can foster children's developing narrative understanding.

Lessons in thievery: Selecting stories for classroom telling

Stories can be drawn from all manner of sources. I would love to be able to say that I learned this or that story sitting at the feet of an old woman as she unfolded the traditions of her people to her gathered family, but sadly I am usually dependent on my collection of story books (picked up on travels, yes, but rarely found at the feet of the elderly), and stories that I hear from other storytellers. In this chapter we look at the way in which we, as busy professional people, can identify and adapt stories for classroom use.

If we were simply considering using stories from collections of folk tales, this would be a relatively simple process. Developing a storytelling approach across the curriculum, however, adds a layer of complexity. When we look for suitable stories, we are not only looking for discrete folk tales, myths, legends etc., but also historical accounts, scientific processes and works of art that lend themselves to the storytelling approach.

In his book *Speaking Out, Storytelling and Creative Drama for Children*, Jack Zipes eloquently sets out the condition of the storyteller:

> The best storytellers are thieves and forgers. They steal their tales from everywhere . . . Sometimes they steal tales from their own experience that they revise, adorn, and dress in such a way that those who might have witnessed the real incidents would never be able to recognise them. Storytellers appropriate their stolen goods, make them their property, and re-present them as if the goods were their own material, which, in many ways, they are because storytellers always forge the tales they steal anew.
>
> (2004: 35)

A skilled thief is, of course, discerning about the quality of the goods they purloin. Once we have looked at the range of narratives that can be appropriated for classroom storytelling, we will then develop selection criteria that will help us narrow down the search. Having set some rules by which we can select a story, we then consider how someone else's story – stolen goods, perhaps – can be adapted and owned, ready for representation.

Story selection – developing skills in thievery

In Chapter 1 we looked at story as the fundamental way in which humans represent themselves and their experiences to each other and, indeed, to themselves. One consequence of this is that the world is full of stories, and we are constantly being bombarded with competing narratives.

Types of narrative

At this point, it is worth laying out the generally agreed categories of story that you might come across in the search for a classroom tale.

Fable

A short story that points to a moral, and in which the characters are often animals. These tales fall into two categories: in the first, the animals remain as animals and display characteristics of their species (e.g. the traditional Scottish tale 'The Fox and the Wild Goose'); in the second, literary form, animals replace human characters and show human behaviours (e.g. Beatrix Potter's *Peter Rabbit*).

As a subset of fable, pourquoi stories ('why stories') explain the characteristics of animals or features in the observable world. They are often related to creation myths, but they lack the grand sweep of mythology and are often humorous. They can range from the Australian Aboriginal tale of how the dishonest (and soft-backed) oyster rolled into a fire during a fight and ended up with the hard ash covering his back (see Reed, 1998: 99–100), to the story of the spire that jumped from the church tower to the ground (where it can still be seen) in surprise at a young couple who wanted to get married in the Kentish village of Brookland, which was known for the loose living of its people (see Westwood and Simpson, 2005: 375).

Myth and legend

Children are often confused between myth and legend, and to be truthful the line between them is often blurred. Legends are traditional tales involving heroes and heroines, which (although overwhelmingly fictional) are told as if they have an element of truth; myths are generally concerned with supernatural beings and seek to explain the natural order, or the problems of human existence. In her encyclopaedic work *Mythology for Storytellers*, Josepha Sherman lists seven categories of myth:

- cosmic or cosmological myths (also known as creation myths);
- myths of birth and life;
- myths of sex and procreation;
- myths of death;

- myths of rebirth;
- myths of the gods;
- myths of the heroes.

(2003: 2–3)

If we accept a that legends lie somewhere between myth and historical fact, it is easy to see where the confusion between myth and legend is located (particularly in relation to Sherman's final category, 'myths of the heroes'). For instance, on the basis of the above definitions, should the adventures of Heracles (Hercules) be considered myth or legend? Clarification is provided by Sherman, who suggests that the heroic role in a society's mythology is to provide a 'culture hero . . . a codified image of that society's ideals' (2003: 3), which places our archetypal Greek hero firmly within the mythic bracket. The legends of Robin Hood, on the other hand, dwell 'somewhere between myth and historical fact' – although there is something of the 'culture hero' in the tales.

Religious story

Although, in technical terms, religious stories form a subset of myths and legends (overlapping with parables/moral tales), their separation here is deliberate and strategic. By religious stories, I refer specifically to those tales that are a part of living faith traditions and consequently require a deal more careful handling than the myths of ancient Egypt or the legends of King Arthur. This is explored in Chapter 8.

Folk tale

Folk tale is a broad term used to describe a short tale, originally derived from oral tradition, reflecting the culture and values of the societies from which it originates. They include fairy tales and fables, as well as tales of mystery and ghost stories that grow out of local traditions.

Fairy tale

The term 'fairy' tale is misleading, as such stories are often notable for their lack of 'wee folk' and sometimes are simply stories intended for children. Fairy tales form a subset of the wider genre of folk tale and generally, although not always, include magical and/or supernatural elements. The best known collections are by Charles Perrault (1697) and the Brothers Grimm (2007). In his original tales, Hans Christian Andersen (published between 1834 and 1872; Tatar, 2008) moves the fairy story into the literary realm, giving an authorial voice to stories which, although his own invention, were based on established themes in folklore.

Saga

Referring to myths and legends of Nordic origin, characterised by episodes of heroic deeds, sagas were originally quasi-historical narratives of a (usually) extended nature.

Although not sharing the historical references of the Scandinavian tales, the term 'saga' can be used to refer to an extended story in which a central character (or characters) experiences a series of adventures.

Parable or moral tale

Related to the fable, the parable is a short story intended to make a moral point or to reinforce values. The most famous parables occur in the New Testament in the teachings of Jesus; however, such moral tales can be found in other traditions and in contemporary writing. The use of parables drawn from faith-based sources is explored in Chapter 8.

Historical account

Although essentially non-fiction texts, historical accounts are often presented in story form. In his introduction to the final volume of his collected stories from English history, Robert Lacey says:

> I believe passionately in the power of good storytelling, not only because it is fun, but because it breathes life into the past. It is also through accurate narrative – establishing what happened first and what happened next – that we start to perceive the cause of things, and what influences human beings to act in the noble and cruel ways that they do.
>
> (2006: 3)

It is important to remember that every historical account is a story that, although based on fact, is told from a particular perspective – the writer has decided which facts are salient and which are superfluous. The teacher who tells a story from history engages in the same process; this is explored in Chapter 7.

Joke or humorous tale

There are many sources of extended jokes, where a story makes an unexpected turn for humorous effect. Children love the language play and the logical games that are played in such stories – often trying to construct their own.

Riddle and conundrum

Linked to jokes, riddles and conundrums are, at their simplest, snatches of narrative that play with our knowledge of language and our understanding of narrative structures. In extended and literary form, they appear as mystery and detective stories.

Process

Although not strictly speaking falling within the notion of story, scientific (and other) processes can have a narrative coherence which is explored in Chapter 9.

Works of art have not been mentioned explicitly in this list, but visual art, music and dance may all convey stories that fit into all the categories above, the narrative being discerned by the viewer/listener even if not articulated by the author of the work (storytelling through and in the arts is explored in Chapters 10–13).

Selection criteria – stories waiting to be told

> If one lesson can be learned . . . it is that each person must learn to recognize for himself or herself what kind of stories are best to tell. This is something no teacher or guidebook can hope to do well – to select stories for others to tell – except perhaps as a classroom exercise.
>
> (Pellowski, 1977: 177)

Despite Pellowski's discouraging words, several authors have provided lists of tales suitable for telling, and examples of story types are often included in instruction books on the art of storytelling. Several writers have also formulated lists of criteria on which to base story selection. Such criteria, of course, reveal as much about the person who sets them, and their own context, as the stories they seek to analyse. In *The Art of the Storyteller*, the pioneering Franco-British storyteller Marie L. Shedlock suggests that the following should be avoided:

1. Stories dealing with analysis of motive and feeling. . . .
2. Stories dealing too much with sarcasm and satire. . . .
3. Stories of a sentimental character. . . .
4. Stories containing strong sensational episodes. . . .
5. Stories presenting matters quite outside the plane of the child's interests, unless they are wrapped in a mystery. . . .
6. Stories which appeal to priggishness. . . .
7. Stories of exaggerated and coarse fun. . . .
8. Stories of infant piety and death-bed scenes. . . .
9. Stories containing a mixture of fairy tale and science.

(1915: 33–43)

Although I hope that I have managed to avoid 'priggishness' and 'infant piety', I have been guilty of telling stories that would fall into just about every other classification (my favourite tale to tell, *Frankenstein*, would be damned on three counts at least). Prohibitions such as Shedlock's reflect the child-oriented literary output of their time, which either did not fulfil the author's idea of childhood, or had been the basis of unfortunate experiences of storytelling.

The approach I am advocating here is not to prohibit any class of story, but rather to set out criteria that are intended to serve not as stone-cast laws, but as guidance based on personal experience (and frequent mistakes). It is crucial to remember, however, that the search for stories suitable for storytelling is not a search for the perfect story as we receive it (in print, speech or other media). It is the search for the story that has the potential to be transformed, owned and presented afresh.

Personal resonance

The most important piece of advice comes from Theresa Grainger's (now sadly out-of-print) book *Traditional Storytelling in the Primary Classroom*, where she emphasises the need for a connection between the storyteller and the story they intend to tell:

> The most successful stories are those which have real meaning and significance for the teller, since unless the tale is in tune with the teller it will not work well. A teacher's enthusiasm for a story is infectious. It allows the story to be 'sung' creatively and fosters commitment from the audience, enticing them to listen, wonder, feel and respond. . . . Finding tales that are waiting to be told, that the storyteller really wants to share, for whatever conscious or unconscious reason, remains important.
>
> (1997: 147)

That phrase – 'finding tales that are waiting to be told' – is central to the search for a suitable story. Of course, it may be difficult for some teachers to imagine mustering sufficient enthusiasm for processes such as the water cycle (evaporation – condensation – precipitation) in order to create a tale that is 'waiting to be told'. However, the storytelling teacher who uses narrative across the curriculum needs to have a level of sympathy towards the story on which they are basing their telling – whether that be the water cycle or the Norse myth of Ymir's skull forming the sky and his blood the seas (see 'The Giant's Skull' in Hoffman and Ray, 1998). This sympathy does not need to be sentimental – the rhythmic and never-ending narrative of the water cycle can have an appeal, and the myth of Ymir opens up metaphors for the living world that few traditions possess. In the end, as Ellin Greene and Janice Del Negro assert:

> The storyteller must take the story from the printed page and blow the breath of life into it. This cannot be done unless the story has meaning for the one who is telling it, because children are quick to sense one's true feelings about a story. The storyteller, then, must enjoy the content, mood, or style and must have a desire to share this enjoyment.
>
> (2010: 59)

The communal nature of storytelling has already been discussed, but the teacher's role as the principal storyteller in the classroom community of storytellers, as the primary conveyor of meaning, has to be comfortable with the chosen story – there needs to be a personal resonance from the moment when the story is encountered, through the process of adaptation, to the point where it is unfolded with the children. At this point, ownership is dispersed among the community and the story becomes part of a shared experience – storyteller and author Sandra Pollerman records a simple formula from the indigenous people of Australia that encapsulates this idea of the tale waiting to be told:

> Story hide behind rock. Wait 'til good teller come along. Then story jump in teller's brain so quick . . . So quietly . . . Teller think story his own idea!
>
> (2001: 20)

Clearly defined characters

The French philosopher Paul Ricoeur suggests that story 'describes a sequence of actions and experiences done or undergone by a certain number of people, whether real or imaginary' (1984: 150), placing human agency at the heart of narrative. Writing on the power of personal narratives, Daniel Taylor suggests that it is the characters of a story, rather than the plot or language, that we remember (cited in Haven, 2007: 77).

The character of oral storytelling, however, does need to be differentiated from its literary counterpart. It is usual in the tradition of the novel for the main characters to be subtly shaded, with complex internal lives and motivations that determine the directions they take. In the oral tradition, characters are more akin to archetypes – model character types, which can be identified in some form in every tradition of storytelling. Many lists of these archetypes have been compiled, often in pairs that represent binary opposites (Table 3.1).

It is this binary opposition that enables clear contrasts between the different character types without lengthy descriptions – they provide a narrative shorthand through which the imagined world can be populated quickly. The folk tale tradition (which is the heartbeat of oral storytelling), in which archetypal characters are painted in black and white, is reflected in the 'broad brush-stroke' approach to character found in much of children's literature, simplicity aiding the comprehension of young readers.

It is not always possible to find stories for use across the curriculum that are populated with clearly defined characters, but in order to make a suitable source for storytelling, the potential for making clear distinctions between characters needs to be there.

Thematic integrity

The deep meaning of stories (traditional and otherwise) greatly exercises writers on both the nature of narrative and the craft of storytelling. It is perhaps unnecessary for the teacher to search through the canon of literary criticism in order to make a judgement about the underlying themes of a traditional tale, but there does need to be an awareness of the messages that stories carry. Steven Swann Jones suggests that fairy tales (specifically) fall into three major thematic categories:

the psychology of the individual, the sociology of the community, and the cosmology of the universe. In other words, fairy tales can be seen as telling us about

TABLE 3.1 Character archetypes in the oral tradition – binary opposites

GOOD	BAD
Prince / heroic young man	Monster / beast (which can be transformed)
Princess / virtuous young woman	Crone / witch
Innocent / faithful child	Selfish / resentful (step)parent
Wise old man / woman	Fool
Faithful servant	Trickster

our own feelings and psyches, as instructing us how to conform to society's expectations, and as offering spiritual guidance about how to see our place in the cosmos

(2002: 20)

Combining Swann Jones's 'major categories of human experience' with a recognition that, as storytellers, we ultimately have control over the thematic content of the stories we tell can provide us with a set of three simple questions when considering whether or not a story is suitable for classroom use:

- What does this story say, or could it say, about the individual?
- What does this story say, or could it say, about society?
- What does this story say, or could it say, about how we experience the world around us?

With these questions, we can ensure that our storytelling has a secure thematic heart which has integrity. In my own work, I could be telling stories for in excess of an hour, choosing themes from world folklore. With many European stories (as provided in their literary form) presenting women as either passive or scolds, I am always careful to ensure there is a balance by adjusting the narratives to include positive female characters. The dangers of presuming to alter the central theme of a narrative through such adaptation are explored below, but the important thing is to remember to ask not just what happens in a story, but what it is about and what it will do.

These three questions allow us to include the thematic core not only of folk tales, but also of historical accounts and scientific processes. A retelling of the story of the Spanish Armada may have as its theme the survival of the small (if not quite powerless) nation of England in the face of the overwhelming force of the Spanish Empire in the second half of the sixteenth century (understanding both society and the world around us). Alternatively, it could be the strength of character of Queen Elizabeth I, monarch of England, as an individual. In science, the construction of a narrative of the water cycle could have as its theme the different states of water, or the continuous flow of Earth's processes (understanding the world around us).

A coherent narrative

In Chapter 2, I argued that for a story to be coherent, it needs to have an underlying structure, or meta-narrative, in which the *actants* (forces that direct the narrative) are interrelated. These actants are categorised as:

- **subject**: the character around whom the narrative turns;
- **object**: that which the subject wants to achieve or acquire (this could be a person, an object or an attribute);
- **sender**: the person(s) or force(s) that moves the subject to seek the object;
- **receiver**: the person(s) that benefits from the subject's successful quest for the object;

- **helper**: the person(s) or force(s) that aid the subject in their quest for the object;
- **opponent**: the person(s) or force(s) that oppose the subject's completion of their quest for the object.

Sometimes you can read a short story and feel that there is something that you have missed because it doesn't 'hang together'. This will often be because of either the absence of one of these actants or, alternatively, such a multitude of similarly characterised persons and forces within the narrative that it is hard to identify their function in the plot (picking up the point about clearly defined characters). When working with scientific or mathematical processes, historical accounts and, of course, works of art, there are frequently either too many characters or missing actants, and in such cases you need to have a sense that this can be rectified without altering the narrative so that it is no longer true to its source. In many cases, it is not too difficult to allocate actantial functions that are not apparent in the original text, but you do need to be aware of how your adaptations may affect the meaning of the narrative.

Linguistic comprehensibility

The point made above, that the search for suitable stories is the search for potential, needs to be reiterated. Fabulous tales are often to be found in folklore collections that are not aimed at primary-aged children, but it is possible to see how suitable and effective language could be woven to recreate a story that is age-specific. It needs to be remembered that the language of the printed page is not the language of speech. Each of us has our own patterns of speech, our own rhythms and cadences as we talk; to give voice to a printed story is to graft ourselves onto the words of someone else. Stories are there to be adapted and 'forged anew', which gives the teacher/storyteller the freedom to alter the language level of the story, to simplify it or, on occasions, to make it more complex.

Linguistic comprehensibility is about more than vocabulary; it is about the way the spoken word holds the narrative and patterns it. A story is understood through moments of tension and release, prompting introspection or communal laughter, which are created through the crafted use of language and non-verbal skills. Opportunities to employ imagery and metaphor – those moments where there is a 'clash of meanings which creates a crisis for the hearer or reader' (Hughes 2003: 88) – should be noted and exploited. With repetition as a key characteristic of folk tales, linguistic motifs and phraseology should be identified, along with places where onomatopoeia and rhyme could support the expressive qualities of the language. The original story (for example, a historical account) may contain none of these devices, but if it is a narrative worthy of telling, then you, the storyteller, should look for opportunities to mould your language and introduce devices such as repetition, rhyme, imagery and metaphor to evoke a coherent world that is not here, and a time that is not now.

Appropriateness to students' developmental level

Although a number of authors provide guides to which styles of story appeal to different age groups (for example, Greene and Del Negro, 2010: 61–64), and such recommendations can be useful for the lower age range, I would like to suggest that when fairy stories are restricted to children at Key Stage 1 and lower Key Stage 2, they are not serving the needs of older children and young people. Horrific tales such as Mr Fox (the English version of 'Bluebeard') work well with children at the middle to end of Key Stage 2, who revel in gore, but may be completely inappropriate for children at Key Stage 1; conversely, the same children who enjoy such tales of mass murder will also respond well to more 'infantile' tales, such as 'The Three Billy Goats Gruff' (I have regularly told versions of the 'Hare and Tortoise' with sixth form students at secondary school) – the key is how they are told.

Cultural relevance and inclusion

Viewing literature and story as a window or mirror is an established metaphor. As a window, story shows 'us' the world that is not 'us', it broadens our experiences and suggests that there are alternative lives to our own. As a mirror, story shows us to ourselves – that is, of course, presuming that we can recognise ourselves within the narrative.

Storytelling presents opportunities to use tales from all over the world in the classroom that are relevant to broader classroom activities. By building our own language around the narrative frame, we are not restricted to collections of stories for children, but can tap online resources and collections of stories aimed at adult reading levels. This wealth of material allows for reflection on the cultural inheritance of the children that we teach in our storytelling. In a paper on inclusion in the children's literature of South Africa, Leoné Tiemensma comments that 'to choose a good story from a particular culture and to tell it well, is in a sense to honour that culture' (2010: 4).

The principle of inclusion and cultural relevance is applicable at a simpler level. Swann Jones identifies one of the common characteristics of fairy stories as 'presenting modest protagonists with whom we can identify' (2002: 75). Cultural relevance, then, extends to using stories in which children can place themselves and their own experiences, however, these experiences do not need to be concrete; children understand abstract concepts such as loyalty and betrayal from a young age (Egan, 1986).

A curriculum link

Despite the title of this book, I would not make a clear curriculum link a condition of choosing a story for use in the classroom. Sometimes there is no further justification needed than 'this is a good story and the children will enjoy it'; however, if the aim is to support a particular area of the curriculum, then stories should be chosen because they have a direct bearing on the children's learning and not simply to provide a distraction.

A socially constructive message

The notion of a 'deep level' of meaning in story is explored in Chapter 8. It is, however, important to note from the start that stories are not value-free – they come out of particular cultures, and they are being used as part of a particular approach to pedagogy in the classroom. We need to take an analytical stance when choosing stories and ensure that we are not promoting values of intolerance or injustice.

Finding suitable stories

Faced with the array of possible sources for classroom storytelling, I suggest the following process, which reduces the amount of time that is wasted in the search for a suitable tale.

- First make your choice of story collection. Consulting the internet without using 'intelligent' searching (restricting the search criteria) will result in an almost over-whelming selection of stories. It is often more helpful to look in themed collections of stories, which may be based on a particular cultures (e.g. Native American), a type of story (e.g. creation myths), or a topic (e.g. stories about the stars). The choice will be based on a need to support the curriculum, to find material with a specific cultural relevance, or to find a tale with a socially constructive message.
- Do not limit yourself to children's versions of stories. When looking for a 'tale that's waiting to be told', seek something that expresses itself in language with which you are comfortable and which speaks to you. When you retell the story to young people, you tell your own version and the language is then tailored to their needs.
- Scan the contents or the index and see if there is a title or reference that catches your attention.
- Speed-read the first and last paragraph (or two) of a few stories. This should enable you to identify the main protagonist, gain a sense of where the narrative story is going, and perhaps discern the theme.
- Read through any tale that seems to arrest your attention more than the others, but do not be afraid to reject it based on the suggested criteria. Then try the next story, and so on until you find the story that will suit your needs.
- Having found a story (or process, account, or work of art) that appeals as the basis for storytelling, the next stage is to adapt the story and make it your own.

4

Forging the tale anew: Adapting the story for classroom telling

Once a tale that is *waiting to be told* has been found, it needs to be 'forged anew' (Zipes, 2004: 35); in other words, re-formed. Storytellers do not read other people's words aloud, they tell their own stories – tales that have been shaped by them to suit their style of telling, and the community with whom their story is to be shared. In this chapter, we look at how to take an existing narrative and form it so that it is coherent in the retelling, and can be told in language that is owned, but not memorised word for word.

Ownership or memorisation

One of the significant hurdles to be overcome by the busy class teacher who wants to use storytelling is that of story memorisation. The method of adaptation advocated in this chapter is based on a structuralist approach to narrative, so that the act of memorisation is applied to a few key elements of the narrative, which are then bound together, and given expression, by language that is flexible and responsive to the needs of the hearers. Such an approach may be contrasted with writers who advocate repetition and rehearsal of stories so that the language itself is secured in the memory.

The National Strategies' *Talk for Writing* materials (DCSF, 2008a) have already been mentioned in relation to their approach based on repetition and imitation. They advocate the use of recordings from which to learn stories (though not word for word). This is followed by an equivalent process of repetition in the classroom, so that children can learn the same story. However, in emphasising the role of repetition and imitation (even if the process does lead to innovation and invention), storytelling is in danger of losing its nature as meaningful exchange. It becomes, instead, concerned with a narrative that is to be memorised and faithfully performed in a predictable format. At the very least, storytelling ceases to be seen as a natural way in which we organise information and express ideas, and becomes dependent on a process of perfection prior to performance; at worst, there is a danger of a story becoming stale, and storytelling a chore.

The approach taken here is based on an ownership of narrative; although it is directed primarily at the teacher as storyteller, it can easily be applied to developing children's own stories and storytelling skills. With appropriate support, children are capable of remembering narrative structures and retelling them in their own words from Key Stage 1, and the second part of this book provides worked examples of how to engage children in storytelling. Doug Lipman suggests that 'A thorough under-standing of a story's structure is the most solid foundation for any attempts at memorizing' (1999: 101). His method is based on visualisation as a starting point and, for children learning a story from their teacher, the para-linguistic elements of voice, movement, use of space and use of artefacts help to create a series of images in the child's head that supports the ordering of plotted events. Starting from the same premise as both Lipman and Pie Corbett (DCSF, 2008a), that the initial stage of adaptation is visualising a story as it is encountered (in performance or print), the process suggested here is:

- find a story that you want to tell (using the criteria laid out in Chapter 3);
- read the story;
- visualise the narrative;
- discern what is, for you, the theme of the narrative and ensure it is consistent and appropriate
- decide on the point of view you will take (whose story is it?) and ensure the tale has a coherent narrative (with the actantial functions filled; see Chapter 2);
- make a note of any important character/place/process names that need to be remembered and ensure the characters are distinct;
- plot the narrative on a storyboard (introduction – problem – events leading to crisis – resolution – end), making sure it is appropriate for the children's developmental level;
- make a note of any phrases, rhymes or figurative language that you want to preserve in your retelling;
- decide how you will bring the children into the time of story, and then return them to the classroom (abstract and coda).

Ensuring internal coherence

Having read the story and visualised the events as they unfold, from this early stage you should be thinking, 'What does this story mean to me?' In other words, does the tale have a theme that will inform the evaluative stance you will take towards the characters and events?

The next step is to decide from whose point of view to tell the tale, and whether it has, or can be adapted to, a simple and coherent narrative from this perspective. On the first reading of 'Little Red Riding Hood', the obvious point of view to take is of the events as they affect the little girl; however, one could tell the story from the perspective of the wolf, or indeed, grandmother.[1]

Having decided around which character the story is going to revolve (subject), the other *actants* need to be identified: object, sender, receiver, helper and opponent. As already noted, many printed versions of short folk tales provide only the barest bones of a story, so the teller will need to generate suitable actants when they are missing in the original. If a story is going to be retold from an alternative perspective, then you will almost certainly need to generate actants from inferences in the original story. If we choose to tell the wolf's story, for example, we would need to ask 'Why does the wolf want to eat Little Red Riding Hood?' A simple solution would be to start the story:

> Once, a wolf was walking through the forest. Although he enjoyed the sights of the forest, such as the light falling between the branches of the trees and the flowers in bloom, he couldn't enjoy the sounds of forest because his stomach was making too much noise. This wolf was hungry!

Many folk and fairy narratives do not give characters significant names, and they are known simply by their character type: the Boy, the Girl, the King, the Witch, etc. However, where character names are provided (and significant), they should be retained. Significance may be determined by the need to respect the culture from which the story originates, or to retain historically significant information. This is clearly the case in scientific processes, where character names are replaced by terms such as *photosynthesis* and *oxygen* (see Chapter 9). However, when character names are not essential, the storytelling convention of using the character type is a useful device. Hence in the Greek myths, for example, those characters who have individual roles, and significant relationships within the narrative, need to be named, while others can simply be given titles such as The King, The Queen, etc. In telling the first stage of the Trojan War, Prince Paris would be named as the subject, Helen as his object, and Aphrodite (the goddess of love) as the sender.

Creating a storyboard

The creation of a storyboard for a simple folk story is not complex (see Chapter 2), but other sources (such as historical accounts) can present a challenge in trying to construct a simple narrative that is suitable for oral retelling. It is here that the actantial narrative schema (Chapter 2) becomes invaluable. The allocation of subject, object, sender, receiver, opponent and helper enables key moments, or turning points, in the original text to be identified and plotted in relation to the identified subject.

At this point, any patterns that give the story an internal rhythm should be identified, such as repeating events or recurring phrases. There are also stories, such as the Grimms' tale 'The Fisherman and his Wife', that are cyclical (see also the Navajo structure in Figure 2.1), so that resolution needs to be related to the introduction. In 'The Fisherman and his Wife', the shrewish wife increases her demands of a wish-granting fish until, finally, she wishes to be God – at this point she is returned with her husband to the poverty that characterised their lives at the beginning of the story.

As with all teaching materials, professional judgement needs to be exercised with regard to the appropriateness of the tale to the children's developmental level. If the main theme of a story is the protagonist's Oedipal desires, then it is probably not going to be suitable for Key Stage 1 or 2 as it stands. However, adjustments may be possible to create a coherent narrative that is appropriate for your particular group of children.

Related to the adaptation and editing of stories is the issue of *bowdlerisation*[2] or censorship. The fear of violence and sexuality has led to what might be referred to as the 'Disneyfication' first of European folk traditions, and now of other cultures. Although some blame may be laid at the door of the 'Magic Kingdom', Disney has simply been the most successful of many forces promoting a romantic notion of childhood and society which, it can be argued, has little relevance to the world as children experience it – or, indeed, to the world of traditional stories. We like to forget that Cinderella's ugly sisters had their eyes pecked out, that Snow White's stepmother danced to her death in red-hot shoes, and that Manypelts was sought in marriage by her own father.

In his important work on the Freudian interpretation of fairy tales, *The Uses of Enchantment*, Bruno Bettelheim theorises that children have violence, monsters and desires deep inside their subconscious. The role of the folk tale, he suggests, has been to give an imaginative language to that violence, and to place both monsters and desires in a context that serves society's structures. Adults often think that the cruel punishments meted out to antagonists in fairy tales upset and scare children unnecessarily. Quite the opposite is true: such retribution reassures the child that the punishment fits the crime. The child often feels unjustly treated by adults and the world in general, and it seems that nothing is done about it; the more severely the bad ones are dealt with, the more secure the child feels (Bettelheim, 1976: 5). In the same way, these stories reinforce social taboos in a symbolic form – taboos that it may be inappropriate to examine explicitly, but that work on a subconscious level (such as Manypelts and her father's incestuous intentions; Little Red Riding Hood climbing into bed with the (older, male) wolf).

It is possible that the lack of a truly enriched inner life may lead to frustration, which can manifest itself as violence. We must therefore think hard before trimming the extremes from traditional tales to make them more acceptable or politically correct. My own experience as a teacher of children with profound emotional and behavioural difficulties supports the view that children need an imaginative capacity for violence in order to express their anger safely. It must be made clear, however, that such an argument does not justify allowing the young access to violent films or images. These provide disturbing mental images, rather than stimulating an imaginative vocabulary. Visual representations of violence force the child's imagination into a particular predetermined form; the shared story allows the child the freedom to shape their own response. However, sensitivity is still required when telling tales involving violence: too much descriptive detail, and again you force the child into seeing mental images that may be inappropriate or frightening; too little, and the child fails to find a world where right is rewarded and evil pays the price for its crimes.

Forming the language of story

With an emphasis on the teller's expression of narrative through their own language, comprehensibility is in their hands rather than the original text. The language content is something that will change with each telling of the story, and its comprehensibility will depend on the same communication skills that the teacher brings to working with their class. There may, however, be particular figurative language or technical terminology (in the case of scientific/mathematical processes and real-life events) that you may wish to retain. The importance of patterns in storytelling language should be stressed here. Although we are aiming for a conversational model of story-making in which meaning is socially created, the language of storytelling (in its crafted form) is heightened, making use of linguistic devices to enhance and refine meaning. We are trying to emulate the language of traditional tales, which, when coupled with the intimate context of storytelling, 'encourages particularly rich visualisations and makes clear imaginative demands' (Grainger, 1997: 51). Betty Rosen's admonition to teachers for a general failure to use crafted language provides a good place to end this section. Although she is ostensibly talking about teachers as writers (and then as speakers), her words point to our responsibility to model the verbal arts for children. Storytelling provides a perfect vehicle for 'manipulating words for creative ends':

> Few teachers of language . . . actually write – or even consciously talk – creatively, in the way that we expect our students to do. Thus we neither develop our own language as we could nor surprise ourselves by our own skills in manipulating words to creative ends.
>
> (1991: 6–7)

Entering and leaving the story world

There is compelling research on the effect on brain function of activities such as theatre and ritual (Schechner, 1990). These *liminal* (in-between or threshold) experiences enable people to enter a state of 'flow', or what Gardner calls 'a feeling of deep involvement' (2006: 120). Brian W. Sturm's research on the effects of storytelling on listeners (published in 2000) is summarised by Greene and Del Negro:

- a sense of realism (the listeners experienced a story 'as if' it were real);
- a lack of awareness of one's surroundings;
- engaged receptive channels (visual, auditory, kinaesthetic and emotional);
- a lack or loss of control of the experience (feeling transported into the story);
- a 'placeness' (feeling inside the story);
- a sense of time distortion – time seemed to pass faster than chronological time for some listeners, more slowly for others.

> (2010: 49)

This liminality marks the storytelling event as a time apart from the everyday world. The abstract, at the same time as preparing the ground for the narrative that is to come, marks a transitional point that leads the children away from the everyday language forms of classroom interaction and into the heightened language and gesture of story. The coda returns the children to the 'real' world and to more mundane linguistic forms.

Perhaps the most common form of abstract in the European fairy tale tradition is 'Once upon a time', which immediately sets up the hearer for the nature of the story; the equivalent ending, of course, is 'And they all lived happily ever after'. Storyteller Patrick Ryan describes the 'once upon a time state' as the place 'where true engagement with story occurs' (in Greene and Del Negro, 2010: 50). These simple phrases simultaneously bracket the storytelling and signify the teller's taking of the focus (and their returning it to the group at the end of the tale). Through the abstract, the storyteller says 'now listen to me, I am going to lead our thinking, and take us somewhere else'; in the coda, they say 'now we are going to return to the world of the here and now, and I am handing your thoughts back to you'.

There are any number of ways to start a story (the Caribbean 'Crick Crack' is mentioned in Chapter 2 as a story ending, but it brackets the telling and so also occurs at the beginning); and I have often used a short piece of doggerel spoken over a pair of clashing claves to break 'normal time' and move into story time (and then back again). My usual practice when topping and tailing a story is to use a format from storyteller Sandra Pollerman:

This is the story of _____, and this is how I will tell it.

That was the story of _____, and that was how I told it.

(2001)

It is important to remember that few children have had no exposure to traditional stories in some form, and there will often be a very strong sense of ownership of a particular version. When I first started as a storyteller, I was often faced with children who would correct my versions of traditional narratives ('No, that's wrong, the shoe was made of glass'[3]). Pollerman's simple format allows the storyteller to establish that the oral tradition is not fixed, allows ownership of the tale to be claimed, and justifies deviating from the commonly received form of a story (often courtesy of the Disney Corporation). Bearing in mind the emphasis on a shared, communal telling outlined in this book, I usually modify the formula to:

This is the story of _____, and this is how you and I will tell it.

That was the story of _____, and that was how you and I told it.

The Hedgehog and the Devil – a worked example of story adaptation

In this section we will take a traditional English tale (which, although not well known, does have parallels in other cultures, one of which is probably universally familiar), apply the selection criteria, and work through the process of adapting a printed text to oral storytelling.

'How the Hedgehog ran the Devil to Death' was recorded in Worcestershire and first published in 1912.

> A hedgehog made a wager with the devil to run him a race, the hedgehog to have the choice of time and place. He chose to run up and down a ditch at night. When the time came the hedgehog rolled himself up at one end of the ditch, and got a friend to roll himself up at the other; then he started the devil off. At the other end of the ditch, the friend said to the devil, 'Now we go off again.' Each hedgehog kept repeating this formula at his own end of the ditch, while the devil ran up and down between them, until they ran him to death.
>
> (Ella Mary Leather, in Philip, 1992: 395)

Here we have the sketchiest of story outlines. It is a useful reminder that the printed text of a folk tale is rarely transcribed from an oral telling and lacks the detail of the performance (including the non-verbal components). However, tales for the telling can be found as often in simple outlines such as this as in more fully developed literary versions of tales. In fact, such sketchy details make it easier to identify the narrative elements that are essential for retelling – it is quite possible to experience that gut reaction that tells you that you have found a 'tale waiting to be told' even with such scant detail.

For me, this story passes the first test of being a 'tale waiting to be told', and I have worked it up into an interactive piece of storytelling that lasts almost ten minutes. Because of its treatment of the unwinnable race, the tale also fits the selection criteria of relevance to the children's developmental level (the narrative convention of the race being familiar through Aesop's fable 'The Hare and the Tortoise'). There is a cultural relevance, not only with its English setting, but also with the opportunities it presents to draw cross-cultural parallels with versions of race tales from around the globe.[4] The same point also gives the tale a curricular relevance through developing children's understanding of variations within the folk tale genre.

The first of the criteria for testing a tale's suitability is narrative coherence. At first glance, this tale is so short of detail that a satisfying and coherent narrative may be difficult to identify. In fact, the lack of detail means that it is easy to identify the essential elements of narrative. This is shown in Figure 4.1.

Clearly, the subject of the tale is the hedgehog. His object is to win the race against the devil, who is therefore the opponent (in fact, both the devil's fleetness and the hedgehog's comparative slowness are also opposing forces); the friend is the helper. As the story stands, the hedgehog's sender is the wager he makes with the devil – and this is where the storyteller's imagination comes into play by creating a more satisfying reason for the race. The wager can stay, but if we ask the question 'Who or what makes the hedgehog race against the devil?' then the response, 'a wager', creates as many questions as it answers. In my retelling, therefore, the story is set up with the devil appearing to the hedgehog and claiming his soul for Hell – the hedgehog's wager and need to win the race now make sense. What is more, the audience then has an emotional investment in the success (or otherwise) of our hapless woodland animal.

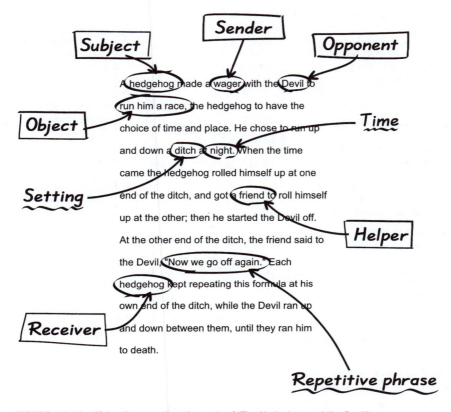

FIGURE 4.1 Identifying the narrative elements of 'The Hedgehog and the Devil'

Having established a more developed form of sender, the receiver (of the benefit of a successful outcome) is the hedgehog himself. Following his initial encounter with the devil, in my version of the story, the hedgehog goes home to his family and explains the situation – the helper becoming his brother.

Having made sure that the narrative is internally coherent, it can be plotted. Using the structure discussed earlier, there needs to be some form of abstract that leads into the story. In this case, the abstract could be as simple as 'and now we are going to have a traditional story from England – not many people know this tale, but they do know one that is very similar, and at the end perhaps you can tell me whether you can remember one.'

The introduction needs to establish the main characters in their time and setting. By opening with a discussion about English woodland and what we might find there, a shared imaginary world can be created in which the hedgehog fits naturally, and the devil represents an intrusion.

Having established the context, the story can unfold. In the adapted narrative (Figure 4.2), the family meeting is inserted as an event before the race itself. The race is represented as one event, when in actuality it should be three or more; given the importance of looking for the patterns and rhythms in stories, the race provides an

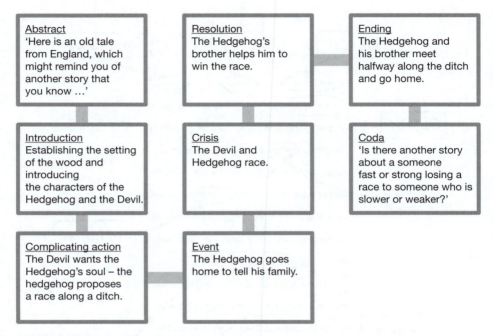

FIGURE 4.2 'The Hedgehog and the Devil' – storyboard

opportunity to create a patterned and predictable sequence at the heart of the story. In the simple printed version, the devil goes back and forth until he is 'run to death'. Although communicating the salient fact that the act of going up and down the ditch was repeated, the original hardly builds tension. How much better to create a verbal formula in which one run of the ditch is recounted, and then the language is repeated. The telling is varied through changing the tone and pace of the repetition, reflecting the devil's growing frustration (the evaluative element of narrative).

In Figure 4.1, the phrase 'Now we go off again' is highlighted as an opportunity for repetition. In fact, I have rejected this chant of the hedgehogs in favour of a rhyme that someone used in their retelling of this tale in a storytelling workshop I was leading (remember the words of Jack Zipes: 'the best storytellers are thieves' – and I did seek permission for this piece of theft). In my retelling, the devil shouts to the hedgehog as he passes him in the ditch:

I'll run you out,
I'll run you round.
To Hell's red fire,
I'll pull you down.

Having set up the question about parallel race narratives at the beginning of the storytelling, the final task is to explore what the children already know of 'The Hare and the Tortoise' and other similar tales. In Egan's terms, the story sets up an extreme comparison between the earthbound, slow hedgehog and the supernatural, swift devil

(Egan, 1992: 72–75). This thematic essence of the race story enables children to construct their own narratives and retell their own versions of the tale.

Summary

We have seen how a simple folk tale can be adapted for live telling by identifying the essential elements of a narrative and how they relate to each other. By combining these elements into a network of relationships, the language of story can be built round it – a language that is flexible and open to adaptation. As an expression of moment-by-moment language, storytelling does not need to be reserved for dedicated and discrete times, but may be used across the curriculum as a natural part of teaching and learning.

5

The craft of classroom storytelling

A word does not start as a word – it is an end product which begins as an impulse, stimulated by attitude and behaviour which dictates the need for expression. . . . a word is a small visible portion of a gigantic unseen formation.

(Brook, 1968: 15)

In this chapter we are going to look at some of the key skills that make up the story-teller's toolkit: voice, non-verbal communication and the appropriate use of artefacts (including puppets) – all things that go into creating that 'gigantic unseen formation'. In the quote above, Peter Brook is referring to the processes behind theatrical per-formance and the words that actors speak on stage, but this notion of the 'unseen formation' provides a useful frame for our discussion of the craft of storytelling. While a storyteller is not a theatre actor (although a theatre actor may be a storyteller), developing a sense of that 'unseen formation' enables us to have a much broader under-standing of communication than simply words spoken.

Storytelling and performance

Recall the following outburst by a student facing a practical storytelling assignment to tell a story with a group of Key Stage 1 children: 'If I'd wanted to do this, I'd have chosen drama, not English!'

It reveals an understanding that places storytelling in a theatrical mould, rather than within the context of teaching, and is common among those who have not consciously used storytelling in their classroom practice. It is a model derived from a notion of 'performance' that is associated at the least with theatricality, and at the last with entertainment. The model of storytelling proposed here, however, is not about per-formance grounded in 'I am' (the actor, the character, the entertainer), but rather a form of social performance in which the whole group (storyteller/teacher and pupils) collaborates to make story together. Note the description of the student's assignment above – 'with a group', not 'to a group'. Not 'I am', but 'we are'.

So, what do we mean by performance in the context of storytelling? Theatre anthro-pologist Richard Schechner refers to performance as 'twice performed' or 'restored' behaviour:

Restored behaviour is living behaviour treated as a film director treats a strip of film. These strips of behaviour can be rearranged or reconstructed; they are independent of the causal systems (social, psychological, technological) that brought them into existence. . . .

Performance means: never for the first time. It means: for the second to the *n*th time. Performance is 'twice-behaved behaviour'.

(1985: 35–36)

For Schechner, then, the term 'performance' covers behaviour that has been pre-prepared, even if not in the sense of the theatrical rehearsal. An alternative interpretation is provided by Erwin Goffman in his seminal work on social role, *The Presentation of Self in Everyday Life* (1959). Goffman suggests that performance by one party is behaviour that is directed at achieving a change in a second party. Between these two authors, we can see how this contentious word 'performance' can cover not only the dancers in a music video and the actor portraying Ophelia in a West End theatre, but also the Year 4 teacher leading their charges to a sounder understanding of long multiplication.

While the teacher/storyteller is not going to represent the character of Ophelia's madness to a paying audience, or gyrate to a heavy bass beat (at least, not in their professional role), they do have to prepare their material, communicating nuanced ideas to enquiring minds with the intention of bringing about change. However, although the skills needed to effect this change have a shared nature with those of the theatrical performer, they are, in fact, simply refinements of those abilities that we bring to everyday communication. There are, therefore, no abilities that are specific to classroom storytelling – the 'performance' skills that we will go on to discuss here are crafted versions of those strategies that we use in our everyday retelling of our lives.

Quality of voice and of movement

Actors and singers train for years to make effective use of their voice, while teachers, who rely no less on their vocal organs, receive lamentably little input on how to protect and use their voice effectively. However, although I am often asked by students to provide practical sessions on voice work, none has ever asked for input on how to use their body effectively. Perhaps they are unlikely to damage their body in day-to-day teaching, but the physical component of communication is no less vital than the voice in contextualising meaning.

Both voice and movement have associated dynamics, as shown in Table 5.1.

These terms have been derived from the 'movement efforts' of Rudolf Laban (1950) and give some indication of the flexibility of voice and movement in communicating expressively. Although the storyteller who has a wide dynamic range in voice and movement has an inbuilt advantage when it comes to expressive performance, those with a narrower range can still express a wide scope of meanings in a narrative, but distinctions between contrasting moods have to be finer and more controlled.

The aim of developing an awareness of these para-linguistic elements of communication is to support the narrative and contextualise the verbal content. To aid a

TABLE 5.1 Dynamics of voice and movement

VOICE	MOVEMENT
Volume: quiet–loud	Magnitude: small–large
Tone: soft–harsh/rasping	Force (weight): soft/gentle–strong
Control: free–bound	Control (flow): free–bound
Pitch: low–high	Speed: slow–fast
Attack, decay and duration: sudden–sustained	Attack, decay and duration: sudden–sustained
Constancy: continuous–fluctuating	Direction: direct–flexible

reflective approach to the storyteller's non-verbal repertoire, I will suggest four story-telling modes (forming the acronym NICE; Table 5.2), which require distinct approaches to voice and movement in order to differentiate between them.

Theresa Grainger suggests that:

> Tales only come fully to life as songs, sung by a storyteller who is sensitive to story structure, meaning and style.
>
> (1997: 154)

This notion of a story as a song to be sung is powerful, and evokes not only vocal dexterity but also physical presence and expression. Being able to differentiate clearly

TABLE 5.2 Four storytelling modes – NICE

MODE	VOICE	DESCRIPTION
N Narrative	Usually third person, but may be first person in personal narratives evoking the imagined world	Events are recalled and sequenced
I Interaction	Second person, within the real world (outside the narrative)	The hearers are engaged in the story and comment on, or direct, the narrative
C Characterisation	First person, from within the imagined world ('as if' behaviour)	The characters speak for themselves
E Evaluation	First person (my response to the narrative standing outside the story while still narrating it)	The narrator lets their hearers know his or her own stance on the narrative (which may include providing supplementary information)

between different modes allows children to hear the difference between questions that are posed to them, and questions that characters ask one another within the story; between the narrative story line, and comments on the form of the story, or details within it.

Space

At times of whole-class (or group) talk, it is common to arrange children on the carpet in front of the teacher. This gathering achieves several things:

- the children's close proximity allows the teacher to address them as one group, rather than several groups;
- the proximity of the children to each other creates a group cohesion, which contributes to individuals' ability to maintain attention;
- teachers can position themselves as the focus of the group's physical attention.

The latter point is crucial. We are slaves to our spines, and our backbones determine that we are our most comfortable when our bodies are balanced. If children sit with their body facing one direction and their head another, the resulting twist in their spine will result in their head wanting to turn to rebalance the body. Consequently, if the body is oriented away from the storyteller, the head will naturally follow. It is important to ensure children are sitting facing the speaker, which cannot be achieved in straight lines – when children sit in rows, their physical orientation is towards the wall behind the speaker, not the speaker him or herself.

When possible, the best arrangement is to have the children arranged in gentle arcs in which everyone's body is focused on the point from which the storyteller speaks (Figure 5.1). From this position, the storyteller can scan the group, making eye contact with everyone and assuring them that they are being addressed personally (and also pre-empting any problem a child may have with concentration).

When I was a student, we were told by Desmond Jones (teacher of mime and physical theatre) that we 'see with our eyes but look with our chests' – in other words, the chest should be oriented towards what we are looking at. By taking this principle into the classroom, children can be encouraged to see the importance of their whole body in speaking and listening – a teacher who introduced the notion of seeing with the chest to her class, encouraging the children to turn their body during discussions, reported that it had a significant effect on their ability to maintain meaningful dialogue. If children are sitting at tables, they should re-orientate their chairs for any period of sustained group talk.

In addition to physical orientation, proximity is a vital component of creating group cohesion. Edward T. Hall (1966) carried out research into how the distance between people both affected and reflected social situations. For Hall, personal distance (the distance maintained in normal interactions between people) is characterised by the participants being able to touch each other without effort; I suggest that this is a useful guide to distance when creating a sense of shared storytelling. The children, oriented

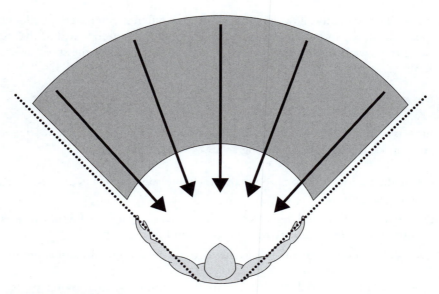

FIGURE 5.1 Group arrangement

towards the storyteller, should be close enough to touch each other on the shoulder without reaching out. The sense of personal contact between the teller and the group is maintained by the storyteller being within reaching distance of the hands of the children on the front row. At this distance, if the storyteller reached out and held the hand of someone in the front row, and then rest of the group created a network of touch, the teller would be connected to everyone, from the front to the back. With this virtual web between its members, the group has a much stronger presence and identity, emotional states are more easily evoked, and moments of tension and release more easily shared.

Absence and completion

Throughout this book, the social aspects and dialogic nature of storytelling are being emphasised. At the heart of this approach is what I choose to call 'absence and completion'. This is a model of storytelling performance that depends on the performer's ability to lead the community into signification, and that has its roots in both ritual and performance theory (Brook, 1968; Turner, 1982; Schechner, 2006; Daniel, 2008). In the storytelling context, 'absence' refers to moments when an element of the narrative is withheld, or a space created in which new information is sought. This absence is controlled by the storyteller: it is intentional, contrived, and aimed at both stimulating students' imagination and, at the same time, leading it along a particular path.

Such absence may be manifested by withholding an easily predictable word or phrase that the students then provide, or by creating a space in which children can supply information needed to complete the story.

It could be visual absence, where a person, place or object is 'seen' by the storyteller in what is empty space – empty until populated by the children's imaginations:

> *Storyteller:* [*focusing their eyes on the space between cupped hands*] . . . and the Lord God looked down at the body of the dead swallow and said to the angels, 'You have chosen well.'

The absence could be one where an everyday object gains new significance through the way it is manipulated in the storytelling:

> *Storyteller:* The fisherman rowed his little boat out into the blue sea . . . [*blue cloth is rippled to signify water*]

In the following section, we will look briefly at each of these forms of absence in turn, and the completion that they enable.

Verbal absence (closed)

Although the closed response makes few demands of children, it does serve as a valuable tool in the armoury of the teacher and storyteller. By providing opportunities to participate in the verbalisation of the story where responses are restricted (such as joining in with a predetermined sequence), children are given a chance to take part in the storytelling in the sure knowledge of success.

> *Storyteller:* The fisherman caught nothing and so he tried again. He lowered his net into the water once more, but again he caught . . .
> *Children:* . . . nothing!

The required response here is clear from the use of the word 'again': the children know 'nothing' is the expected response. Although the children are engaged in simple comprehension and recall (in other words, lower-order thinking), they are being assured that their listening is valued and that the story cannot continue without their contribution. This emphasis on shared telling also resonates with Peter Brook's rejection of the very word 'audience' because of its suggestion of passivity. Rather than watching a play, Brook prefers the French notion of 'assistance' (1968: 156), which has connotations of active contribution to the event; if the children *assist*, the storytelling cannot take place without their participation.

Returning to the closed response, there are some simple guidelines to its use:

■ the moment of absence should be framed by clear verbal and non–verbal cues (the latter may include a slight raising of the pitch of the voice in expectation, accompanied by lifting the eyebrows to open the face, suggesting reception);

■ the expectation should be clear and unambiguous.

There is a danger in overdoing such closed questioning because it is the simplest form of student participation, and therefore the one most likely to generate a successful response. If it is used too often, the session itself becomes closed and predictable, nothing but a series of tests of compliance.

Closed questions can also be used to construct a pattern of thinking that helps the coherence of the narrative. For instance:

Storyteller: The fisherman let down his net into the blue sea and he caught. . . . ?

Answers to such a question can range from the obvious, 'a fish', to the surreal, 'a piano', and sometimes the lateral: 'a cold'. In fact, the sought-for answer of 'nothing' regularly appears. Care should be taken to value the fact that the child is contributing, even if their answer is not the one sought; they didn't know the answer that you were seeking, but why should they? Although there is a 'correct' answer ('nothing'), the aim of the question is not to find it; the aim of this process is to initiate a playful atmosphere and build up an imaginary world within which the story plays out. In this example, the suggestions of marine life both populate the setting of the ocean and contrast its bounty with the fisherman's empty net.

Verbal absence (open)

Instead of asking for simple one-word answers to supply details of the story, the story-teller can ask open questions, inviting the children to contribute to the group under-standing of the story:

Storyteller: Then the crab decided to use his brain to win the gold. What can you tell me about a crab?

In this example, the students help each other to build a mental picture of the animal character. This socially constructed picture will then inform how they hear the story about the crab. There are details that are necessary for the story to continue (in this case, that crab shells are normally hard), but there is less of a sense of trying to find the right answer, and rather that of building a picture in which descriptive language can be employed and children encouraged to go beyond one-word answers. It should be emphasised that such times of contribution should, above all, be dialogic and draw on children's knowledge of the world and their evaluation of the events being recounted.

Reflecting students' contributions

When the students have provided information to build the kind of mental picture discussed above, their contributions to the story should be, where possible, reincor-porated and developed during the narrative. When the storyteller recalls a child's contribution to the narrative (and indicates that they know which child made it), the shared nature of the construction of the story is emphasised. For instance, in retelling Oscar Wilde's 'The Happy Prince', the children could be asked to suggest what the swallow's brothers and sisters see when they fly to Egypt (such as pyramids, temples, palaces and tombs). Later in the story, these suggestions can be reincorporated into the telling:

Storyteller: 'My Prince,' said the swallow. 'I must now fly to Egypt where I will see the great pyramids, the solemn temples, the gorgeous palaces and dark tombs'.

By doing this, not only is the story is seen to be a continuous whole, but the storyteller is seen to have listened to the children and valued their contributions – contributions that are integral to the story and necessary for its completion. Although it is not always possible to use this strategy, when it is appropriate, it is a powerful technique for generating group ownership of the story and fostering the classroom community of storytellers.

Visual absence

We engage in visual absence in everyday storytelling to illustrate events as we recall them. When describing a misbehaving photocopier, we jab a finger down on the imagined green 'copy' button to suggest to our listener that there is, present, an errant machine. The absence is in the gap between the story world and the real world; the action bridges that gap, providing scaffolding for the imaginative response of the hearer.

Unlike moments of verbal absence, there is no overt invitation to make a contribution in response to visual absence. However, visual absence can make the story world present and take the storytelling community to a liminal point, the threshold between the imagined and the real. In this way, the storyteller can create a king by simply holding a plastic crown over a vacant seat: the way in which the crown is held, the use of gaze and the space given to the chair all build a scaffold for the imaginative response – to see a king who wears a crown and sits on a throne.

By using resonances with actions or material properties (such as rippling fabric for the movement of water, or faceted glass for a precious stone), the imagination is stimulated to 'complete the picture' in order to understand the scene. This process is a form of symbolisation in which the space between the actual and potential is exploited, and without which all but the most literal art forms would be impossible. Because of this, there is potential for children's vocabulary of metaphors to be broadened as their capacity to identify associations between actions or objects is enhanced.

Citing Paul Ricoeur, Graham Hughes defines metaphor as 'a clash of meanings which creates a crisis of a kind for the hearer or reader' (2003: 88). Visual absence creates a place where the literal meaning of space clashes with its signified meaning. Such activity dominates children's imaginative play, in which dolls are endowed with life and sticks take on the qualities of light sabres. This ability to see what may be present in another reality is an act by which that clash of meanings is reconciled and is an essential part of children's accessing metaphor.

Puppets and objects

Storytellers around the globe use significant objects and puppets in their tale telling. In this section, we consider the place of using artefacts in storytelling, and establish some guiding principles for the use of puppets.

Using a physical object (such as a crown) can anchor a story in the here and now, and provide a common reference point for everyone (storyteller included). By using a plastic garden cauldron in telling the West Indian story 'How the Crab got a Hard Back', everyone present knows what the witch's cauldron looks like, its scale, and how it is used by the witch at the centre of the story. Following the pioneering work of Neil Griffiths, *storysacks* have become a feature of many primary classrooms. Griffiths notes that 'By using props, scenery and characters they bring any story to life and provide a highly visual and tactile quality to a storytelling session' (2001: 17).

However, care needs to be taken that objects are not overused. On a purely pragmatic level, it is only too easy to lose focus on the story because of concerns about locating and controlling an object, and if more than one object is used at a time, manipulation becomes difficult and expressive movement is hampered. More significantly, a physical object forces the child's imagination down a particular path – 'not the cauldron in your imagination, but my cauldron'. For that reason, objects should be used only if they are significant, and their significance should be revealed in how they are handled.

Although overuse can restrict children's imaginative responses to a story, objects such as a cauldron have an iconic function in story, standing for their fictional equivalents in the narrative, and therefore can be seen to be related to the illustrations in a book. As such, they contextualise talk, rooting vocabulary to objects, and provide a useful resource to assist children's sequencing of story when working with children with English as an additional language (EAL).

However, it is important to realise that the object in storytelling is not simply a referent for a specific noun, but a locus around which other non–verbal cues contextualise language. The action of lifting the cauldron that accompanies the words 'She cautiously picked up the cauldron' not only locates the noun 'cauldron' in the object, but the verb 'lifting' and the adverb 'cautiously' in what happens to it. There will, of course, be meanings attached to the object, and the way in which it is manipulated, which have no direct tie to the language being used but still inform the understanding of the narrative.

Despite the physical presence of an object, however, there is still an element of absence and completion involved: the cauldron is not the cooking pot of a witch, but a garden planter; the stone held up as the statue's precious eye in 'The Happy Prince' is not a cut sapphire, but a faceted piece of glass. The storyteller takes these iconic representations and endows them with an imaginative reality which should be respected and maintained throughout the storytelling. The faceted glass is a sapphire for the time that the imagined world is evoked in story; once the children have returned to the real world, then it can be glass once more. The reasons for this consistency of approach are discussed below in relation to puppets, but apply equally to the use of other objects and artefacts in storytelling.

Bringing objects to life: puppets and puppetry

Puppets are a special class of object in which the absence in need of completion is that of life: 'Whenever someone endows an inanimate object with life force and casts it in a scenario, a puppet is born' (Blumenthal, 2005: 11).

The puppet is a lifeless object until manipulated in such a way that its movements are familiar as those associated with independent life. It therefore can be seen that, just as classroom storytelling is a crafted version of everyday exchange, puppetry is the equivalent of children's play when toys are endowed with life. Giving life to a puppet is as fundamental as sitting Teddy and Tyrannosaurus Rex at the table for tea. The difference between puppetry and play is that the storyteller is engaged in performance (a prepared act that is intended to have an effect on its audience), not simply populating their own imagined worlds.

Because the puppet's life is independent of the storyteller, it provides an additional focus that can draw in children who otherwise have difficulties in sustained listening. It also feeds the imagination, not only allowing the child to share in adult play, but also providing a model for their own play.

Puppets are usually representational and provide a form of iconic shorthand for the characters they represent. This enables the whole group to share an image of a particular character, and is particularly useful when a story is populated with a lot of characters as it helps to differentiate between them. Linked to the discussion above in relation to objects in general, puppets provide useful illustrations for children with EAL, contextualising the language of character. When characters talk to each other in a narrative, the listeners have to differentiate between the meaning of 'he said' (referring to the first character) and 'she replied'(referring to the second) – the puppet allows the hearer to identify the participants in a narrated exchange and develop their mental picture of the characters' actions and interactions. As Datta (2000) notes, children with EAL who are reluctant speakers can feel comfortable speaking when they are given the opportunity to use a puppet. Perhaps the puppet provides a distancing tool: I am scared to make mistakes with my language, but the puppet is not me, and if it makes errors, they are not mine. The psychic distance that exists between any actor and the role they play is enhanced by the separation of the storyteller and the puppet (Kaplin, 2001) – the creation of this distance is one of the main aims of the puppetry strategies outlined below.

Continuing the theme of children using puppets, opportunities should be provided for them to explore different forms of puppet in their own storytelling. Children, from Key Stage 1, are quite capable of separating themselves (as narrator) from the puppet (as character), and switching between third-person narrative and first-person characterisation. For the child, the puppet (as noted above) not only may provide a mask that permits a level of both verbal and non-verbal expression that would otherwise not be seen in talk, but also may support a developing awareness of narrative conventions (such as speech and characterisation).

Choosing puppets

There are five main classes of puppet (Table 5.3), although they sometimes appear in hybrid form.

There are a wide range of puppets available both in shops and online. Individually crafted puppets tend to be very expensive, but commercially produced hand and finger puppets can be purchased for a few pounds. In addition, soft toys can be adapted with a little sewing know-how, and children and adults can make puppets from a variety

TABLE 5.3 Five main classes of puppet

PUPPET	DESCRIPTION
Hand or glove	Usually fabric and easily obtained in toy shops, they are sometimes made to suit particular hand sizes so that those intended for small children cannot be manipulated by adults, and *vice versa*.
Finger	The cheapest form of puppet, and widely available in story sets. Easy to manipulate, but very limited in movement and, therefore, expression.
String or marionette	Manufactured in a variety of materials, these can be stunningly beautiful and have the potential for a range of expressive movements. They are, however, very difficult to keep tangle-free in the classroom. Simple marionettes with only a couple of strings tied in (such as those from Rajasthan) lessen the chances of tangling.
Rod	Limbs controlled with rods rather than strings and therefore without the danger of tangled strings. Wooden Indonesian rod puppets are readily available.
Shadow	Made from leather or card; have the disadvantage of needing additional equipment (screen and light source), although children can operate their own puppets against a window.

of materials, from old socks to the cardboard tubes inside kitchen paper rolls. Indeed, the most expensive puppet is of no more use than an old sock with buttons for eyes unless it is capable of being manipulated effectively. The old sock, cardboard tube and small-world figurine have much to recommend them, besides cheapness, as they create a larger space between the representational and the real: the beautifully made copy of a bird of paradise may provide an accurate representation, but it leaves less room for the imagination to function than a less sophisticated form.

Puppet manipulation

As discussed above, the distinctive quality of puppets is the illusion of life that is independent of the manipulator. Four simple strategies in puppet manipulation can help create this semblance of life for both adult and child storytellers:

> articulate – isolate – resist – respect.

Articulate

Most puppets are capable of very limited actions – the operator should explore the possibilities and discover what non-verbal communication can be achieved within the constraints of the puppet's construction. Hence glove or hand puppets can often gesticulate with their arms (as can rod puppets), while finger puppets usually cannot be articulated beyond moving the puppet's whole body.

Isolate

People hold their gaze on things that are unfamiliar, and ignore that which is common and everyday. By directing your gaze at the puppet, you are looking on it as something separate from yourself, something in which you are interested. Observers will follow your gaze, so by looking at the puppet you will make it the centre of attention. Returning eye contact to the observers will draw their attention from the puppet, which allows you to place it out of sight (or retrieve it) without such actions breaking the narrative.

Isolation is also reinforced by respecting gravity. A glove that happens to be shaped like a tortoise can sit in the air – as a glove, it covers a hand and is supported by an arm. A tortoise that has a life independent of the manipulator, on the other hand, has weight and needs to be supported on a surface if it is not to fall to the ground (the free hand can often provide this support).

Resist

In order to suggest life in the puppet's movements, the operator needs to inject tension through muscular opposition or resistance in the hands. Muscular resistance is the tension you feel in your hand when you unscrew a tightly closed jar; by tensing the muscles in this way, the puppet appears to have an internal musculature and has to put effort into its movements. This applies particularly to hand puppets, which can have a tendency to move in a series of loose waves in the absence of resistance.

Respect

During moments when a puppet is representing an autonomous life, avoid handling it as an inanimate object (unless you are breaking the illusion for a purpose). If the pig is an autonomous animal one moment, and then is simply a furry glove covering a gesticulating hand the next, the observers have to negotiate very rapidly between the imagined and the real. When the illusion of the puppet is broken, the imagined world which it inhabits is simultaneously disturbed. It is the same reason that the faceted glass, mentioned above, should remain 'as if' it is a sapphire as long as the story world is evoked.

If children are using puppets as they develop their crafted storytelling, it is important to establish that the objects with which they are working are puppets, not toys. Awareness of this distinction can enhance the child's manipulation of both the puppet and narrative conventions (which can become blurred in the free flow of play).

Conclusion: sharing storytelling competence by allowing children to become critics, sages and seers

The term *competence* in the context of performance is borrowed from sociology: to have a competency means possessing the necessary skills to complete a task, and a context within which those skills can be successfully employed. For the actor playing Ophelia, her competency lies in her ability not only to learn the lines, but to express them in voice and action in a way that is consistent with the character. Further, although she may be able to deliver her lines as the character of Ophelia with great expression, the actor's ability to portray the character of Ophelia is also dependent on her fellow actors treating her as Ophelia, and the audience's recognition of her in role as the person of Ophelia. In other words, even the high-end performance of classical theatre is dependent on more than the abilities of the actors – on a shared communal response to the performance event. In the classroom community of storytellers, a sense of communal competence lies at the core of the storytelling.

The idea of memorising a story by learning its structure rather than a script can be daunting for some people, but avoiding fixed language and developing the skills necessary to be flexible in retelling a narrative are vital to dispersing competence. If a teacher repeats a story word for word, action by action, without reference to the children with whom the tale is shared, the balance of competence lies squarely with the teller and their ability to perform a text to a passive audience; the children's competence is restricted to the ability to listen – or (worse) to manifest those behaviours associated with listening. In a classroom community of storytellers, the storytelling is characterised by a more even spread of the necessary competencies. The teacher/storyteller still needs a commitment to communicating the narrative ideas, but the children 'assist' (to reiterate Brook) with the storytelling, which becomes dependent on their contributions. This means that the telling could not happen without the interventions of that particular group of children, in that particular context, emphasising the communal nature of classroom storytelling.

In this chapter, we established storytelling as a form of social performance which is pre-prepared and aimed at bringing about change (echoing both Schechner and Goffman). In order to do this, the storyteller needs to be aware of the messages they communicate, not only in their words, but also in the way their voice is used and through their movement, so that these para-linguistic elements of communication need to support the narrative and differentiate between characters, moods and different forms of exchange (telling, questioning, discussing, etc.). Both the language of story, and the crafted use of voice and movement, can be enhanced with the use of objects or artefacts (including puppets). These can help define moments in story and give it a physical presence in the gathering, but (as with voice and movement) care needs to be taken not to allow them to interrupt the flow of the tale or distract from its meaning.

In addition, we have considered some of the ways in which the storytelling competency can be shared, so that children and their ideas can be incorporated into the storytelling. Through the strategy of absence and completion, children are able to comment on the narrative, predict outcomes, make suggestions to augment the story, and offer critique. As seers, children predict the trajectory of the narrative, identify problems likely to confront the characters and discuss possible solutions. In commenting on and critiquing stories, pupils not only step outside the imagined world to judge its internal coherence, but respond to the devices used to communicate the narrative (which will include the non-verbal as well as the linguistic). This notion of story as a locus for summary, critique, prediction and projection is essential to the core message of communal storytelling.

It is through understanding the factors that contribute to storytelling competence, and how they can be shared, that the story truly becomes a moment of social exchange.

Storytelling across the primary curriculum

6

Words, words, words: Storytelling, language and literacy

The publication of *Speaking, Listening, Learning: Working with Children in Key Stages 1 and 2* (for schools in England and Wales; DfEE, 2003) highlighted the role of children's talk in the classroom and the need for teachers to take a strategic interest in developing children's skills in speaking and listening, alongside those of reading and writing. Further, the profile of speaking and listening was raised by the publication of the Early Years Foundation Stage (DCSF, 2008b), which placed a strong emphasis on the role of talk (including story) in developing children's response to, and understanding of, language and the sounds from which it is constructed. Few would deny that storytelling plays an important role within children's experiences of speaking and listening, and in this context professional storytellers may continue to enjoy demand for their services in school. However, if storytelling is to achieve its potential as both a model of talk and a means of engaging children with narrative, then it cannot be regarded simply as the preserve of the specialist teller of tales. This book advocates storytelling as a key pedagogic skill across the primary curriculum, but it is in the area of developing children's language and literacy that it has its most immediate and apparent relevance.

Developing language through storytelling

The storytelling teacher is engaged in a complex activity that demands a variety of skills related to both narrative awareness and communication competence, which they model for the children in their class. The role of imitation in language acquisition is well documented (Wood, 1998; Smith *et al.*, 2003) and is visible in how people pick up vocabulary and phraseology from family, friends and media (the spread of the use of the word 'like' as a linguistic filler provides a good example; see Hitchens, 2010). The child who experiences the story told (as opposed to the story read or the story memorised) is therefore experiencing the possibilities of personal and expressive speech, aspects of which they can incorporate into their own language.

In Chapter 1, attention was drawn to the differences between reading and telling stories, but this discussion is worth expanding in the context of its role in literacy teaching. When we read a book to children, we show them the potential of written language, of its crafted and perfected (well, at least edited) state. If we interject during our reading, then children hear our words in juxtaposition to those of the author, for there is always an opposition created: this is the story, the work of the author; this is me, your teacher. Even if we highlight particular linguistic devices, we are stepping apart from the text and examining it from the outside, we are saying 'look how clever the writer is – perhaps you could write like this too'. For the storyteller, there is no such dichotomy: the words of the story are the words of the storyteller; the words of interjections and asides are the words of the storyteller. When a storyteller tells their story, they are saying, 'listen to how I use the language between us, these are some of the possibilities of talk.' Interruptions in the story flow to reflect particular phraseology can be the starting point for a discussion in which children generate their own forms of language and incorporate their ideas back into the story, creating a rich dialogue between teacher and children.

The very purposefulness of the exchange when a story is told means that children are able to experience listening for sustained periods. Of course, many children are well practised in behaviours that suggest that they are listening when internally they have drifted to another shore altogether. However, dialogic storytelling has the potential to engage children as active listeners. When I was working in schools, it was not unusual for teachers to remark that they had never before seen their pupils (as young as Year 1) sit attentively for seventy-five minutes, and my response was always the same – it's storytelling, that's all. If my approach had been to 'perform' stories in front of the children, I am certain that they would have lost interest within minutes; but in aiming to foster a sense of communal storytelling, I hoped to give the children the sense that the tale told was something to be created together through shared language. For, in order to participate in the told story, children have to be active listeners so that they can intervene appropriately in the narrative. They have to understand the conventions of narrative, apply them to content they hear, and look for possibilities for the way in which the narrative will develop. There are clear links here to developing the higher-order reading skills of prediction, sequencing, characterisation, analysing and making inferences, as well as drawing on their own knowledge of other stories (Barrs and Thomas, 1993; Fisher, 2006a). Jacqueline Harrett summarises the benefits of storytelling for children's listening skills:

> Storytelling techniques do not only enhance the speaking and listening skills of children. These methods help change children from superficial, deceptive or even inattentive listeners into more participatory and reflective listeners and learners who may also become more creative thinkers.
>
> (2009: 39)

Beyond listening skills, research supports the role that storytelling can play in developing the complexity of children's thinking and language use. Kendall Haven's book *Story Proof* (2007) provides a meta-analysis of current research into the effects of storytelling and narrative thinking (his research also features strongly in Chapter 11). Contrasting storytelling with story reading, Haven cites research in British primary schools by Susan Trostle and Sandy Hicks, comparing the effects of storytelling with story reading, which shows that 'while both showed strong positive effect, storytelling was superior to story reading for student vocabulary development and for comprehension' (Haven, 2007: 114). Similarly, an earlier survey reveals evidence that storytelling (over reading) leads to improved comprehension in listening and reading, develops linguistic fluency, and improves understanding of story concepts (Isbell *et al.*, 2004).

Elizabeth Grugeon's cites feedback from students, following their experiences of telling stories in school, suggesting that story has a range of effects in the classroom:

- a means of communication and control;
- a means of sharing experience;
- a stimulus for other activities;
- a stimulus for looking closely at language;
- a means of developing expertise as tellers and retellers;
- a means of questioning and discussing issues.

(2005: 66)

Storytelling, then, has a clear place in the teaching of language and literacy, for all the reasons above.

In addition, there is a more mundane aspect of the modelling process that should be recognised: if we expect children to be able to tell coherent stories, using a range of communication skills, then we need to provide experiences of storytelling, and model its various aspects and manifestations. When they tell stories themselves, children work within a structure in which they are able to demonstrate their prowess in language (Bearne, 1998: 153), and experiment with their abilities in verbal and non-verbal communication. As they produce texts that can be moulded and revised in the very act of communication, children's narrative competence grows to the benefit of their reading, and helps them develop what Theresa Grainger calls 'power over the written narrative' (2001: 107). She notes that children's:

confidence, oral competence, memory, vocabulary and sense of self can be positively influenced as they tell tales which entertain others, share cultural understandings, bridge gaps and gain perspectives on their own lives.

(2001: 114)

Further, when children tell stories, they see their language having an effect on others. They have a chance to see how different modes of expression create different effects and the ways in which they can encourage their peers to engage with their narratives. Keiran Egan's work has placed story and narrative understanding at the heart of learning, and he sees the use of language to create imagery as key to the learning process:

The development of the narrative capacities of the mind, of its ready use of metaphor, of its integration of cognitive and affective, of its sense-making and meaning-making, and of its overarching imagination, is of educational importance because these capacities are so central to our *general* capacity to make meaning out of experience.

(1992: 64)

Further, the role of language in cognition means that, in supporting this creative, expressive and accurate use of talk through storytelling, we are helping children to construct what Alexander refers to as 'the true foundation of learning' (2008: 9).

Storytelling in teaching phonics – contextualising language

The debate over the place of systematic synthetic phonics (SSP) as the principal method of teaching early reading is what might be best described as 'live'. In this short section, I address how storytelling can be incorporated into the teaching of phonics to create opportunities for sustained and meaningful exchanges of language.

This concern with the nature of the talk that takes place in SSP is clearly based on a social–constructivist approach to language development, in which language is fundamentally a social phenomenon and cannot be understood in isolation from its purpose as meaningful exchange (Goouch and Lambirth, 2007). The cognitive–psychological approach that lies behind SSP suggests that by initially limiting children's learning to structured and systematic exposure to the building blocks of the decoding process, their ability to access meaningful exchanges is enhanced. This allows the most common patterns in written English to be established in the child's memory before they are applied to more complex combinations of sign systems (Solity, 2003). By applying storytelling to the teaching of phonics, those concerned with the seemingly mechanistic approach of SSP can create sustained times of meaningful exchange without undermining the systematic aspects of the synthetic phonics programme.

Paulo Freire describes reading thus:

Reading does not consist merely of decoding the written word or language; it is preceded by and intertwined with knowledge of the world. Language and reality are dynamically interconnected.

(in Larson and Marsh, 2005: 41)

In story, reality and language meet in meaningful exchange, and by placing children's learning within purposeful two-way communication, at the same time as key skills are being learned, the social purpose of reading and talking is not lost.[1]

One of the common features of phonics programmes is the creation of word banks to exemplify either particular phonemes (the sounds that make up spoken English), or grapheme–phoneme correspondence (GPC), compiled by children responding to flash cards or bags of objects. A growing bank of GPCs may then be reflected in staged readers, in which children are not expected to read any word that they have not been taught to decode using SSP apart from those that depend on memorised sight vocabulary (termed 'tricky' in *Letters and Sounds* and 'red' in Ruth Miskin's *Read Write Inc.*).[2] During the oral component of this process, teachers and children devise sentences that demonstrate the target phonemes, such as 'I love shaking vinegar on my fish and chips'. Such activities are aimed at developing children's phonological awareness and ability to identify phonemes in spoken English. However, sentence-level work engages children with a rarefied form of decontextualised language which, while drawing on immediate SSP learning, has little relationship with the majority of the language that they use (or are exposed to), and would seem to contribute little towards developing children's ability to engage in sustained and coherent discourse.

In a survey of writing on the differences between contextualised and decontextualised language, Julia Scherba de Valenzuela (undated) identifies several features that mark out the latter as 'classroom language' and that this is 'used to convey novel information'. In other words, it is the language of formal English, in which referents are clarified within the text without the need for external reference points. Contextualised language, on the other hand, is typical of everyday conversation, and is dependent on shared knowledge and the use of para-linguistic cues, such as pointing to an object to concretise a reference to 'it', or looking at a person to indicate who 'she' is. Because of these characteristics, contextualised language is more readily accessible to children than decontextualised, both in speaking and in listening (the referents are readily apparent without linguistic definition). Sentence-level work, while perhaps useful in embedding grammatical construction in early reading, creates short, self-contained, bursts of meaning that not only lack the space/time cues used by contextualised language, but also are unrelated and non-sequential and therefore fail to provide mutual semantic support. To ask children to invent sentences that exploit a particular stage in developing SSP is to ask them to combine words that, although sharing focused spelling patterns, invariably have no semantic connection with one another beyond the length of the sentence.

Research by Ryokai *et al.* (2003) on the responses of young children to storytelling suggests that experiencing storytelling encourages children to construct their own stories, which helps develop their handling of decontextualised language. In their experiment, a 'virtual peer' (a computer-generated talk partner) modelled storytelling and, importantly, storytelling language, which enabled children to use sustained decontextualised language structures. The modelling aspect is clearly important, but the use of narrative ensures the child is not faced with a mechanistic selection of words based on syntactical appropriateness alone, but rather has semantically coherent choices that build to an overall story structure.

As I have stated, story is the natural way in which we organise information; to use storytelling in this context is not to add a further linguistic burden to children's SSP learning, but to work with the way in which they naturally construct language and relate to the world around them.

The Leading Partners in Literacy project at Kingston University was built on the premise that by modelling the language of story, the teacher could embed the phonemes which were being used to focus particular elements of SSP in a meaningful context. This could then lead to children creating their own short (but coherent)

narratives, which represented sustained discourse and the meaningful creation of contextualised language.

The project asked students (once they had observed the teaching of SSP) to teach
a phoneme in which they told a story to the children; on the following day, the
children told their own versions of the same story. During this phase (on the third
day), children were engaged in a shared writing session through group storytelling.
In my role as the tutor for this project, I recorded a demonstration video of short
stories in which specific stages in the learning of SSP were targeted (the final videos
were produced by Kingston University and distributed on DVD; earlier versions of
two of the tales may be found at www.storytent.co.uk).

An outline of the methodology by which consonant digraphs (ch, sh, th, wh) were
embedded into an English folk tale is given below as a worked example.

'The Old Woman and her Pig': /ch/, /sh/ and /th/

'The Old Woman and her Pig' is a nonsensical Mother Goose story that has a very
simple structure, is strongly sequential and very repetitive. An edited version is given
below.

> An old woman was sweeping her house, and she found a little crooked sixpence.
> 'What,' said she, 'shall I do with this little sixpence? I will go to market, and buy a
> little pig.'
>
> As she was coming home, she came to a stile: but the piggy wouldn't go over
> the stile.
>
> She went a little further, and she met a dog. So she said to the dog: 'Dog! bite
> pig; piggy won't go over the stile; and I shan't get home tonight.' But the dog
> wouldn't.
>
> She went a little further, and she met a stick. So she said: 'Stick! stick! beat dog!
> dog won't bite pig; piggy won't get over the stile; and I shan't get home tonight.'
> But the stick wouldn't.
>
> She went a little further, and she met a fire. So she said: 'Fire! fire! burn stick;
> stick won't beat dog; dog won't bite pig; piggy won't get over the stile; and I shan't
> get home tonight.' But the fire wouldn't.
>
> She went a little further . . .
>
> [*the intervening events can be discerned from the last few paragraphs of the story:*]
>
> She went a little further, and she met a cat. So she said: 'Cat! cat! kill rat; rat
> won't gnaw rope; rope won't hang butcher; butcher won't kill ox; ox won't drink
> water; water won't quench fire; fire won't burn stick; stick won't beat dog; dog won't
> bite pig; piggy won't get over the stile; and I shan't get home tonight.' But the cat
> said to her, 'If you will go to yonder cow, and fetch me a saucer of milk, I will kill
> the rat.' So away went the old woman to the cow.
>
> But the cow said to her: 'If you will go to yonder haystack, and fetch me a
> handful of hay, I'll give you the milk.' So away went the old woman to the haystack
> and she brought the hay to the cow.

As soon as the cow had eaten the hay, she gave the old woman the milk; and away she went with it in a saucer to the cat.

As soon as the cat had lapped up the milk, the cat began to kill the rat; the rat began to gnaw the rope; the rope began to hang the butcher; the butcher began to kill the ox; the ox began to drink the water; the water began to quench the fire; the fire began to burn the stick; the stick began to beat the dog; the dog began to bite the pig; the little pig in a fright jumped over the stile, and so the old woman got home that night.

Central to the concept of using storytelling in the teaching of phonics is a shared commitment to both the teaching of SSP and the story as story – the tale has a value of its own (and is therefore worth engaging with), it is not just an excuse to reiterate target consonant digraphs. The narrative therefore needs to be well structured and the internal relationships coherent (even in a tale as simple as this). The story structure is outlined in Figure 6.1.

Given this structure, it is a relatively simple process to replace the events (which involve a dog, stick, fire, water, ox, butcher, rope and rat) with a similar (but shorter) sequence that incorporates vocabulary which emphasises the consonant digraphs /sh/, /ch/ and /th/.

To do this, a table of possible words is generated (Table 6.1).

When I told this tale, the story bag that accompanied it contained objects both to support the narrative of the story and to provide mnemonics for the phonics. Puppets

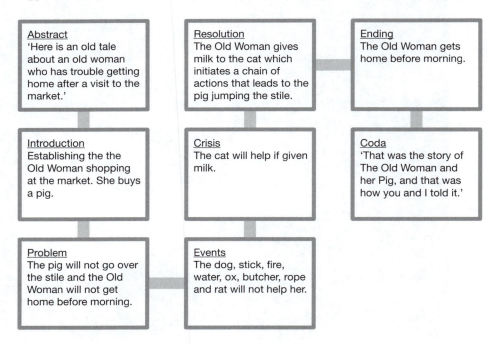

Abstract
'Here is an old tale about an old woman who has trouble getting home after a visit to the market.'

Resolution
The Old Woman gives milk to the cat which initiates a chain of actions that leads to the pig jumping the stile.

Ending
The Old Woman gets home before morning.

Introduction
Establishing the the the Old Woman shopping at the market. She buys a pig.

Crisis
The cat will help if given milk.

Coda
'That was the story of The Old Woman and her Pig, and that was how you and I told it.'

Problem
The pig will not go over the stile and the Old Woman will not get home before morning.

Events
The dog, stick, fire, water, ox, butcher, rope and rat will not help her.

FIGURE 6.1 'The Old Woman and her Pig' – storyboard

TABLE 6.1 'The Old Woman and her Pig': /sh/, /ch/ and /th/

DIGRAPH	NOUNS (AND PRONOUNS)	VERBS	ADJECTIVES
/sh/	shoes, she		shiny
/ch/	chicken, chair	chase	
/th/	this, that	think	

of a pig and cat provided referents for characters already within the story structure (Figure 6.2), and a shiny shoe (a Christmas decoration) and a chicken puppet allowed me to relate the target digraphs to concrete objects. Utilising the words generated above, we can create the new version of the story in which, while the old woman cannot persuade her pig to jump the stile, the cow will not push the pig over the stile because she is too busy showing off her shiny shoes, and the dog will not bark at the cow because he is too busy chasing a chicken around a chair. The digraph /th/ is incorporated into the story as a deliberately abstract element so, when the old woman

FIGURE 6.2 The old woman's perfectly pink pig

comes across the cat, it is persuaded to stop 'thinking about this, and thinking about that' and, instead, agrees to scratch the dog, who barks at the cow, who pushes the pig, who jumps over the gate (I replaced 'stile' with 'gate' to avoid placing additional linguistic hurdles in the children's way when they came to tell the story for themselves). Needless to say, the old woman does get safely home before morning.

In this new version of the tale, the storyboard remains almost the same as the original, while the internal structure of the tale remains intact (shown in Figure 6.3). The story needs the sending function of the old woman's desire to get home before morning to give the story a trajectory and to ensure the narrative has momentum. All the time, the intransigence of the pig is her main opponent, with the cow and the dog becoming helpers through the agency of the cat.

The story can, of course, be freely adapted by the children, so that the old woman may ask the help of a 'fish who is frying some chips' – the nonsensical nature of the episodes remains a challenge of decontextualising language, but it is purposeful and set within a coherent narrative frame.

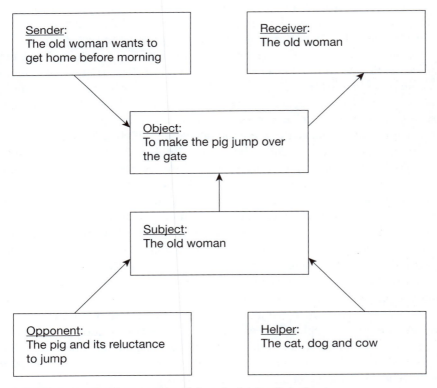

FIGURE 6.3 'The Old Woman and her Pig' – actantial narrative schema

Storytelling and children with English as an additional language

A large proportion of my own work has been with children and young people who are learning English as their second, third or fourth language. One of my earliest engagements as a professional storyteller was to tell folk tales from around the world to a room of 150 young people who had been learning English for three months – I have to confess to thinking that their teacher was insane to set up a seventy-five-minute session for these children, when their vocabulary alone would be far too limited to understand the content of the stories. I could not have been more wrong. Yes, vocabulary was limited; yes, the command of English grammar meant that anything but the simplest construction failed to convey its full meaning – but the para-linguistic components of storytelling, which essentially recontextualise language that is otherwise decontextualised, enabled the children to follow and enjoy the tales to the point that my visits became an annual feature of the school's English language teaching. Non-verbal elements, including tone of voice, rhythm, pace, the use of puppets and artefacts, and participation by the pupils (all of which provide referents for the linguistic content of the story) are essential for children with English as an additional language (EAL) as they develop a relationship with English through story (Datta, 2000).

In addition to the support provided by the performative aspects of storytelling, the very nature of story as a meaningful exchange of ideas supports the understanding of children with EAL. It is a human trait to expect a verbal exchange to have meaning. If an utterance doesn't make immediate sense, the hearer will 'search for or invent an interpretation of the utterance to give it sense' (Bruner, 1986: 28); in addition, the structural aspects of narrative provide a scaffold for that interpretation.

In Chapter 2, we looked at the efforts of Propp (1928) and Greimas to create a grammar of story. More recently, Christopher Booker (2004) has used the Jungian psychology of the archetypes to suggest that all stories, from the folk tale to Russian realist novels, can be reduced to seven basic plots: Overcoming the monster, Rags to riches, The quest, Voyage and return, Comedy, Tragedy, and Rebirth. The key message of these various theorists is that story structure is, at the narrative level, predictable within certain parameters, and when contemporary authors eschew these structures (for example, *On the Road* by Jack Kerouac), we understand their text by noting the absence of established narrative patterns. The child with EAL may not have a fluent grasp of grammatical construction or a widely developed vocabulary and command of idiom, but their inherent knowledge of story and narrative structures means that interpretation of the verbal content occurs within an established framework of possibilities (cultural limitations of this are explored below). Wyse and Jones's observation that 'Story telling can be . . . [a] particularly successful method of encouraging the multilingual child to negotiate between more than one language' (2008: 251) recognises the universality of the story form and its potential for inclusive practice.

Beyond the structural aspects of narrative, the common characteristics and patterning of story language also make it a rich resource for children with EAL. By hearing and participating in stories, they are hearing 'models of language which are *comprehensible* but also *beyond what the learners are able to produce themselves*' (Pauline Gibbons in Lewis, 2006: 139–140). Ruth Lewis suggests the following qualities for stories most suitable for storytelling with EAL beginners (although it is clear that she is failing to distinguish between storytelling and story reading):

- those with repetitive predictable refrains or storylines;
- those whose language structure and vocabulary are natural;
- those clearly supported by good illustrations;
- those that span cultural and age boundaries.

(2006: 140–141)

In their paper on narrative learning for children with EAL, Cortazzi and Jin note that narrative patterns vary between cultures, and therefore teachers should be aware of some of the story conventions that children bring with them (2007: 654). (Variations in narrative structure are discussed in Chapter 2.)

Not only should children with EAL be hearing stories, they should also be telling them. The use of visuals and the creation of storyboards, on which key vocabulary and phrases are given, have been found to be very effective in supporting children with EAL in their own storytelling (Cortazzi and Jin, 2007) and Manjula Datta suggests that through learning poems, rhymes and stories, children are given a 'foundation for learning the conventional tunes of meaning structures in the second language' (2000: 236).

Summary

As a discrete area within the curriculum, literacy would seem the natural place in which to explore storytelling, and in this chapter we have discussed the role of storytelling in developing children's capacities in language, including the teaching of early reading. However, this chapter has been placed as the first of those related to curriculum areas for a reason – literacy and language inform everything that happens in the classroom. The oral telling of story in history, art, dance or any subject area will engage children with sustained and purposeful expressive language, which can only enhance their own linguistic abilities.

7

Stories of pipers and tales of tall ships: History and geography through storytelling

In this section, we focus in the ways in which classroom storytelling can enhance children's understanding of the world around them. The potential for the told story to develop children's ability to handle geographical and historical concepts is considered through exploring the sense of place in story and the ways in which events are held in narrative.

Location, location, location: developing geographical understanding through storytelling

When asked 'what are the essential elements of story', both children and adults usually begin with character, immediately followed by setting. We have already looked at how stories travel the world in different forms, each version particular to its culture, place and time. This cultural and geographical specificity provides an opportunity to explore how setting can influence the way in which a plot is unfolded and why narrative variations exist.

In Chapter 4, we looked at the process of adapting the traditional English tale 'The Hedgehog and the Devil' for classroom telling. This variation of the race theme (most familiar in Aesop's tale 'The Hare and the Tortoise') is located specifically within the English countryside, and in the process of communal storytelling children can be led in constructing a verbal picture of the setting with its trees, fields, hedgerows and animals. Similarly, if we are telling the Xhosa version of the same story (another hare and tortoise race), we imagine the veldt of South Africa, and pool our knowledge of the flora and fauna of southern Africa in order to contextualise the tale. Here is revealed a tension between the universality of the themes of traditional (and other stories) and the specificity of particular tales: although 'The Hedgehog and the Devil' could be reset in South Africa (there is a species of hedgehog native to southern Africa), 'The Hare and the Tortoise' makes no sense in the English countryside (unless the tortoise has escaped captivity).

This tension presents us with the opportunity both to broaden children's understanding of the morphology of the traditional story (the building blocks, shape and variations of a tale) and to introduce them to unfamiliar places and cultures. Referring specifically to myths and legends, Donna Rosenberg comments that they:

> were created for the purpose of conveying cultural values, attitudes, and pride, and they are tied to specific locations in time and space through the historic settlements of their people and the actions of their heroes.
>
> (Rosenberg, 1997: xxxii)

In addition to myths and legends, traditional stories in general reveal much about the cultures that tell them: social and familial structures, habitation, traditions and history.

If, as an example, we look at the Xhosa variation on the well-known folkloric theme of the transforming husband or wife (familiar in the Perrault tale 'Beauty and the Beast'), we find the younger of two sisters following her sibling's path through the forest to find the terrible Snake Chief. Because she has followed custom, and shown respect to her elders, she does not suffer her sister's fate of being eaten by the five-headed monster serpent; instead, the younger sister's deference and adherence to tribal tradition enables the Snake Chief to be transformed into the handsome human chief that he was before suffering the curse of an evil spell (see 'The Snake Chief' in Arnott, 1962). Through this story, the community of storytellers can explore the importance of tradition to the Xhosa people, as well as the place of music and dance in their culture (the younger daughter travels with dancers and drummers as custom dictates); when retelling, I use a simple Xhosa vocal motif of *Hamba kakuhle* ('go well'), which we can all sing, to punctuate points in the sisters' journeys (see Chapter 13). However, when telling a tale from a culture other than one's own, it is important to do nothing that will diminish the value of the tale; we should also avoid any attempt to create 'cod' speech patterns or ritual behaviours that imitate other cultures. In the end, I am a middle-aged white man who lives in Surrey, and it is far better that I own my identity and do not pretend to be something that I am not. That does not mean that we can't dramatise, characterise and create our own moments of ritual – but this is 'the story how we tell it', not as we imagine people from the culture of origin have told, or continue to tell, a tale.

While story may perhaps seem a natural way in which to represent unfamiliar cultures and settings, it can be overlooked as a means of representing the school's culture and its setting, despite emphasis in recent curricula on developing children's awareness of the world by starting with their own environment. Yet story is the way in which we represent the world – including that part of the world in which we reside. Further, story is the means by which we make causal connections between events that happen within that world.

The following section provides an outline for a session that uses both teacher and child storytelling in which a traditional story is re-set in the environment of the school.

This scheme has been used for a range of groups, from children in upper Key Stage 2 to postgraduate university students.

'The Piper of Newtown'

Versions of the story of how a piper leads a town's children away, never to return, can be found all over Europe, the most familiar being the German 'Pied Piper of Hamelin'. Each regional variation is particular to its place so that, while in the German tale, the piper leads the rats to drown in the river and the children into the mountains, the English version, 'The Piper of Newtown', is particular to its setting on the Isle of Wight. Anyone visiting the island will find little in the way of mountain ranges, but a lot of coastline communities, so in this story, the rats drown in the harbour, while the children are lost in the forest that used to cover the island. This localisation of the tale reflects the way in which stories travel and are adapted so that people can represent the world as they find it, and not just listen to stories of distant lands and wonder at their strangeness. In this way, the great storytelling motifs that express the human experience of love, loss, courage and virtue can be seen to represent experiences that relate to 'our' lives, and not simply to the lives of others: 'their' lives.

The suggested activities (see Figure 7.1) are grounded in the notion of the classroom community of storytellers. The session is structured so that, starting with the story told by the teacher, children develop and tell their own, localised, versions of this well-known tale. Through this process, the children engage with the geographical and topological language of location, and devise and tell their own versions of the 'Pied Piper' story in which the setting is not only clear, familiar and accurate, but determines the outcome of the narrative.

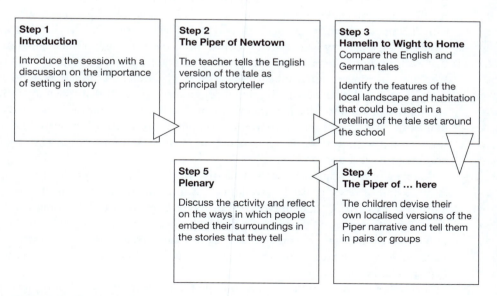

FIGURE 7.1 'The Piper of Newtown' – session outline

The session should take between forty-five minutes and an hour to complete at its simplest level; there is potential, however, to extend activities with additional background research and story refinement. Of course, the teacher will need some time to prepare the story of 'The Piper of Newtown' if they are going to tell it – although simply reading the story would serve to initiate the children into the structure and motifs of the narrative, it would not provide a model for their own storytelling.

The climax of the session is when the children tell their own versions of the story, and they should support each other in the devising process. Although the final task is individual, in the sense of each child becoming the principal storyteller for their tale, they can be encouraged to make use of absence and completion strategies so that their storytelling becomes a communal act.

Step 1: Introduction

Introduce the session by asking the children to identify the essential components of a story (characters, setting, time, a problem, etc.). Remind them about the importance of setting, and ask for some typical examples of settings that would occur in different genres of story (fairy tale, adventure, horror, science fiction, etc.). Tell the children that they are going to hear a story (do not tell them the title) and that they should listen carefully for all the references to the setting.

Step 2: 'The Piper of Newtown'

The teacher/storyteller tells the story of 'The Piper of Newtown', the original version of which can be found in Joseph Jacobs's *More English Fairy Tales* (1894) (online at www.projectgutenberg.org). Remember that this is storytelling, not story reading – it is essential to model effective storytelling practice if the children are to construct and tell their own versions of the story.

Adapting this story for telling presents challenges. Although it is easily broken down into discrete episodes (Figure 7.2), we are faced with the problem of identifying whose story we are telling when we come to allocating the actantial functions. Although the title is 'The Piper of Newtown', when I tell the story the subjects are the Mayor and councillors, their object being not only to rid their town of rats, but to do it cheaply. In this model, the Piper becomes the opponent because he wants payment for his services, the Mayor and the councillors' helper being their own ability to dissemble over the payment. In the end, of course, the power of the Piper is too great and, although the object of ridding the town of rats is achieved, the condition of its being done cheaply is overturned with the loss of the town's children. All of these narrative relationships are represented in Figure 7.3.

Once the subject of the narrative has been chosen, and the actantial functions allocated, the story can be learned for telling (the Piper's story could be told if an appropriate actantial schema has been generated). Although an unfamiliar story on the surface level, awareness of 'The Pied Piper of Hamelin' means that the tale will be familiar at a narrative level, and the sequence of events will consequently be easy to remember. It is the level of manifestation that makes this version distinct from its German cousin: the particulars of place, and the turn of events that place dictates.

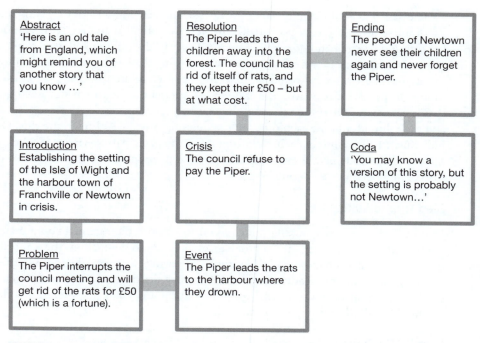

FIGURE 7.2 'The Piper of Newtown' – storyboard

Step 3: Hamelin to Wight to home

In discussing the story with the children, it is important to talk about what they know of 'The Pied Piper of Hamelin' (which may be nothing more than the title). An inevitable question arises as to the meaning of the word 'pied'. Taking pleasure in language is one of the joys of storytelling, and the teacher/storyteller shouldn't be afraid to take diversions into etymology if explanations do not divert too far from the purpose of the narrative. In this case, 'pied' is simply an adjective derived from the magpie: originally meaning a garment that was made of black-and-white patches, it came to mean clothing that was made up of different-coloured patches. As fabric was expensive, pied clothing was an indication that someone was poor – they couldn't afford to buy larger pieces of cloth from which to make clothing. By discussing the word's origin, the relative poverty of the piper is established without the need for further explanation.

Turning to the setting, the children are asked to recall any references to place in 'The Piper of Newtown' (in Jacobs's version the town hall, the harbour, Gold Street, Silver Street, Harbour Road and the forest are all mentioned). To make a comparison with the German version of the story, reference could be made to the section of the Robert Browning poem where the fate of the rats and the children is established:

> Great rats, small rats, lean rats, brawny rats,
> Brown rats, black rats, grey rats, tawny rats,
> Grave old plodders, gay young friskers,

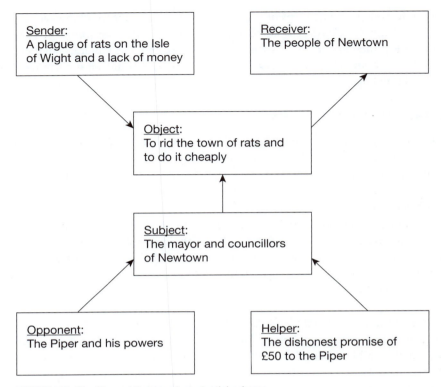

FIGURE 7.3 'The Piper of Newtown' – actantial schema

Fathers, mothers, uncles, cousins,
Cocking tails and pricking whiskers,
Families by tens and dozens,
Brothers, sisters, husbands, wives —
Followed the Piper for their lives.
From street to street he piped advancing,
And step for step they followed dancing,
Until they came to the river Weser
Wherein all plunged and perished!
. . . .
When, lo, as they reached the mountain-side,
A wondrous portal opened wide,
As if a cavern was suddenly hollowed;
And the Piper advanced and the children followed,
And when all were in to the very last,
The door in the mountain-side shut fast.

(Browning, 1842: lines 111–122, 226–231)

By referring to online maps of the terrains of Lower Saxony and the Isle of Wight (perhaps using *Google Maps*, www.googlemaps.co.uk),[1] the ways in which the two stories reflect their geographical settings can be compared. The children can then make suggestions about which features of their environment could be incorporated in a localised retelling.

Step 4a – The Piper of . . . here

The trajectory of this session, and its principal outcome, is for the children to create their own original and local versions of the Piper narrative. The following six-question version of the actantial analysis can be used to scaffold the children's responses.

Who is the story about?

The children need to identify the character(s) around whom events will turn; in other words, who has the problem? Working within a structure that places the commissioning authorities as the subject, this function could be fulfilled by the headteacher and the school governors (always a popular choice); it could be the parent–teacher association or the council, but it needs to be a person or group that is perceived to be in authority.

What is the problem? What starts this journey?

The problem in both Hamelin and Newtown was that the towns were overrun with rats, but the children can choose their own plague (when doing this exercise with teachers in Antwerp, it was decided that the story was about the King of Belgium, who was desperate to get rid of a plague of politicians).

The key point, which shouldn't be lost, is the lack of resources to pay someone to solve the problem.

What do they want to do?

They obviously want to solve the problem, but (and not to be forgotten) to do so cheaply – this then enables a tension to be created between the intended and inevitable outcomes.

If they succeed, who will it help?

This is the motivating force of the story. In Hamlin and Newtown, it is the people who will benefit. In 'our' school, it might be the children or the teachers. This will then naturally lead into the end of the story, as the Piper exacts revenge on the community for lack of payment.

What is working against them?

The force working against the authority figure(s) is the professional nature of the Piper – he (or she) wants to be paid for their services. It should be noted that in the revised story, the Piper need not play a pipe in order to lure the plague away. I have known mobile phone ringtones to be used and, in the case of the Belgian teachers, cash was scattered in the path of the politicians to draw them to their doom.

What is working for them?

The helping device that I have emphasised in my retelling of 'The Piper of Newtown' is the duplicity of the mayor and councillors in agreeing to pay the £50 fee – calculated deception is the means by which they rid themselves of the rats, and seem to do so cheaply.

The discussion outlined above may seem long-winded, but it can take a matter of minutes to explore the different elements of the narrative through a dialogue around these six questions in a group setting. Its value lies in reinforcing the importance of a coherent set of relationships within a narrative, and developing children's awareness of the grammar of story. From here, the children's imaginations can run free. They need to work out for themselves:

- Where is the meeting in their chosen setting?
- What is the price the Piper demands?
- How is the Piper going to lead the rats (or whatever plague is chosen) away?
- Where does the Piper lead them, and how does s/he dispose of them?
- Who does the Piper take away when s/he is not paid?
- To where does the Piper lead their victims?
- How does the story end?

Step 4b – Storytelling

Before the children tell their stories to each other (either in pairs or groups), it is worth reminding them to follow the narrative pattern of 'The Piper of Newtown'/'The Pied Piper of Hamelin', but to include local geographical features, place names and characters to make the story as specific as possible to the locality.

In exercises such as this, it is very easy to become so focused on the content of the story that the performance aspects of storytelling may be lost. Children's storytelling, as much as the teacher's storytelling, must be understood as a live, oral, communicative (indeed, conversational) act; children need to be aware of the dynamics of voice, body language, use of space, use of props, and the application of the principles of absence and completion (even if those words are not used) as well as the narrative structure and linguistic components.

Step 5 – Plenary

Immediately afterwards, reflect on your overall impression of the children's storytelling (see Chapter 6). Remember that the role of the listener is not passive, and that children who may not be the most confident at oral expression can be praised for their active listening – a necessary component of communal storytelling.

Encourage the children to assess each other's stories. This should be carried out *in situ* (sitting with their storytelling partner) and be framed around the criteria described in Table 7.1 (either within the pair, or as a whole group).

TABLE 7.1 Criteria for assessing the stories

Was the story clear?	Were you able to follow your partner's story? Did it make sense?
Could you recognise the story of 'The Pied Piper'?	If your partner told their story to someone from another class, would they say 'I know a story like that'?
Was the setting clear?	Did you know where the story was happening? Did the places join together so that you could imagine moving through the setting of the story?
What references to place were there (and what geographically specific language was generated)?	Our aim was to tell a story set around the school – what locations did your partner mention?
How did the storyteller make the places in the story important?	Your partner could have chosen any of more than a thousand locations around the school to use in the story – how did they make the spaces they mentioned seem important? Did they use adjectives or adverbs to describe them and the ways in which the characters moved through the places? What about tones of voice and gestures?
How were the characters adapted to be appropriate to the setting?	The original story was set in a fishing town; the main characters were the mayor and councillors, the rats, the children and, of course, the Piper. Our story is set around this school; did your partner create characters that belong in and around the school (apart from the Piper)? Did they make you feel sympathy for any of the characters?
Were the fates of the rats and the children tied to the location?	In the Newtown story, the rats drown in the harbour and children are led into the forest – locations that would have been familiar to the people of the Isle of Wight. Did your partner use familiar places and change the way that you see them?

Extension activities

From this activity, the children could develop the story further into geographically related activities:

- create maps of the area, highlight the locations mentioned in the story, and mark the routes the Piper takes;
- lead a small group on a guided tour of the locations, telling the story as a tour guide (this may not be possible in reality, but can work as a dramatised activity in the school hall) – the communal nature of the storytelling is brought out by the group's role as visitors, asking the kinds of questions tourists might ask about the places they visit;

- look at old maps and images, and consider how the story would have to be adapted to the area around the school – 50, 100, 500 and 2000 years ago.

Differentiation

The structure of this session is itself supporting of children's learning. As the narrative level of the story is pre-existing, the child's task is to represent that narrative altering its manifested content (that is, while the language of the story is the child's, the narrative provides a familiar scaffold on which to build their story).

- For those children who need linguistic support, provide maps with key locations marked and that relate directly to the exploratory section in Step 3 (the maps could highlight features that are clearly visible on satellite mapping).
- Have printed copies of the storyboard available for those children who need reminding of the linear structure of the narrative.
- Paired or group storytelling – the children choose the localised elements of the story together and, in the storytelling, take turns to tell different scenes in the sequence. It must not be forgotten that storytelling is a communal activity, and if a teller is struggling to find words, their hearer(s) can support them with suggestions.
- For children with English as an additional language, tell the story as a group with an adult as the lead storyteller, giving the children the opportunity to add the necessary information to make the story local (photographs of the locality with clearly written captions could help here). The adult, as the principal storyteller, has the chance not only to direct the narrative so that it remains coherent, but also to support the group story with non-verbal cues (including actions, vocal tone, rhythm and the use of objects).
- For gifted and talented children, develop the use of specific, geographically related language by providing them with terms that they should try to include within their story – such as the cardinal compass points, references to incline and gradient, and indications of the age of features of the landscape (Victorian, Bronze Age, post-war, etc.).

Storytelling the past: history and the tales we can tell

Geographical understanding is inextricably linked with a sense of how our environment has been shaped by its past, leading neatly to the role storytelling can play in children's learning about history.

My childhood love of history has never worn off, and stories that were populated with kings, pirates, martyrs, scientists and tyrants have stayed with me into adulthood – a personal statement in which some of the tensions within the teaching of history, indeed, about the very nature of history itself, show themselves. Should we teach children tales of the great leaders of history, or concentrate on exploring the lives of the multitude and how the experiences of ordinary people have changed from age to age? Although there is not the space here to enter a debate that is explored elsewhere, and by those who speak with more authority, it is important to acknowledge that the view of history as story is not uncontested. The skills of the historian can be viewed as the ability to engage in

> examination of sources and interpretations in a critical, appraising way to generate theories about their validity and reliability: historical methodology is characterised by scrupulous respect for evidence and disciplined use of the imagination.
>
> (Davies and Donoghue, 1998: 117)

While Davies and Donoghue argue for the place of story in history teaching, they do suggest that the need for children to examine, interpret, appraise and, above all, be critical is in conflict with the potential for them to be cast in the role of passive receivers of a personal interpretation of events. The Finnish sociologist Matti Hyvärinen, in his paper 'Towards a Conceptual History of Narrative', cites the historian Louis Mink:

> Stories are not lived but told. Life has no beginnings, middles, or ends; there are meetings, but the start of an affair belongs to the story we tell later, and there are partings, but final partings only in the story.
>
> (2006: 23)

In other words, the narrative structures that we ascribe to historical events are artificial structures imposed on events that unfold through human encounters – encounters that are lived moment to moment, rather than plotted. All of which returns us once more to Livo and Reitz's assertion that story is a 'way of organizing language' (1986: 5). Historical stories are linguistic frameworks by which we can make sense of events – the storyteller looks for a turning point to fill the narrative function of crisis, and identifies points in the events that make a natural start and a fitting end. As such, the storyteller always speaks from a viewpoint (including some details, excluding others) and takes an evaluative stand, ascribing affective and moral value to events and characters.

Given all of the above, the use of storytelling in history may seem fraught with pedagogical difficulties. If, however, we ask the question, 'how do the problems of partiality affecting the storyteller differ from historical writing?', the answer is, in essence, 'not very much'. Even if, in form, the historian's work may be far more developed, their view of the past remains central to their work – the very act of choosing to study a particular event or period privileges that event or period over others that are not worthy of close study (a point of particular relevance to the classroom teaching of history during times of changing curricula).

For the storytelling teacher, this concern is doubled – not only are they reducing a huge breadth of human experiences to a series of coherently linked events with imposed points of commencement and conclusion, but they are claiming authority as one who can speak without reference to a book. Their standpoint, their evaluation, carries a personal weight that reading a story from a book would not carry Alan Farmer and Christine Cooper (both committed to the role of storytelling in history teaching) cite unpublished 1995 research by Bage when they suggest:

Some fear that stories appear to locate too much power in the hands of the teacher. The storyteller/teacher can oversimplify: can sketch characters as caricatures and complex situations as archetypes of good or evil. Arguably, when the teacher 'takes for granted' the moral basis or outcome of a story or an episode in history, the children learning from it are denied the opportunity critically and democratically to decide their own version or interpretation of what 'this story means or shows'. Storytellers can impose coherence where there is none. They can promote acceptance, close down possibilities and exclude questioning.

(1998: 27)

Farmer and Cooper go on to argue that the teacher, however, is present as a person with a wider frame of historical knowledge than the children they teach, and creating story is a means by which order can be given to otherwise disparate events. As Rosie Turner-Bisset states in her book *Creative Teaching: History in the Primary Classroom*:

The ordering of experience through the sequencing of events in a spoken narrative seems to have a much more lasting impact on the human mind than does a collection of facts and concepts, or even an organised web of linked ideas.

(2005: 87)

Further, it is noted in the 2007 Ofsted report *History in the Balance: History in English Schools 2003–07* that children are weak at 'linking information to form an overall narrative or story'; by constructing historical narratives themselves, teachers are providing a model of conceptual organisation in narrative form. A solution to concerns over the power of the teacher as a purveyor of personal interpretations of historic events is, then, to make our standpoint explicit – when we relate historical narratives, we need to be clear about whose tale we are telling and to recognise the evaluative nature of our storytelling. The examples that follow of the effects of taking different standpoints and contrasting evaluations show how it is possible to use storytelling to lead to meaningful dialogue about the complexity of issues that become woven together to make an engaging narrative.

Having given some consideration to the nature of storytelling and the use of the story form, we need also to consider the content of the tales we use in classroom history. Here, another tension is revealed – between retelling the remarkable and studying the everyday. At the age of six, my hero was Horatio Nelson – his life story was told (with fairly unsophisticated line drawings) on the children's television programme *Blue Peter*, and I treasured any book that had details of his transformation from unpromising, sickly child to Britain's greatest naval hero. Living in the south of England, it was not too difficult for my parents to take me to see Nelson's flagship, *HMS Victory*, at Portsmouth, and I will never forget the experience of learning something of how the ordinary sailors lived (and suffered) – my insight into the lives of the working people, motivated by the story of one remarkable man. A naval hero is hardly representative of the mass of humanity who populated the period and culture of which he is iconic, but it is hard to deny that the stories associated with him are full of the tension necessary to hold an audience. What is more, the life of Nelson is intertwined with the stories of the struggles and triumphs of the ordinary sailors whom he led.

Shortly before his appointment as Secretary of State for Education, Michael Gove stated in an interview with *The Times* that parents would like to see 'children sitting in rows, learning the kings and queens of England' (Sylvester and Thomson, 2010). While I am not a natural apologist for the views of this 'unashamed traditionalist', there is, however, a germ of truth here which has the potential to enrich the classroom teaching of history. Few of us who work in education would see history in terms that can be shorthanded to the kings and queens of England (particularly anyone working in one of the other nations of the United Kingdom), but the 'great' stories of history are compelling. The stakes are high in the game of royal politics, and the conflicts that are played out between opposing and helping forces affect not only the protagonists, but also nations and even continents – heightening the tension inherent in the tale. The struggle of the Saxon farmer to provide for their family is, of itself, fascinating social history, but in the end that family's fate had only limited repercussions. The great stories of generals, queens, revolutionaries, religious zealots and social reformers are important because they pull us into the historic *milieu* which helps to contextualise a deeper and more grounded learning about people who were 'just like us'. The historian Sarah Dunant said in a radio broadcast that her teachers had 'hooked us with the story' and then 'hit us with the real stuff' (in this case the complexity of the English Reformation), and it is this hooking ability of story that is there to be harnessed.[2] A.J.P. Taylor stated that 'we shouldn't be ashamed to admit that history at bottom is simply a form of storytelling . . . there is no escaping the fact that the original task of the historian is to answer the child's question: "What happened next"' (cited in Farmer and Cooper, 1998: 36).

Developing the base skills for history through storytelling

Although extending the knowledge base for history is addressed below in considering the telling of historical tales in the classroom, there are elements of historical understanding and skills that are addressed through working with narrative itself.

Turner-Bisset (2005) suggests that history is understood through three parallel strands: substantive knowledge, syntactic knowledge, and attitudes and beliefs. Substantive knowledge comprises facts and concepts, in turn the concepts can be broken down in to first-, second- and third-order. Bisset describes her first-order concepts as those 'which define the ideas with which history is concerned'. She lists these as: chronology, a sense of period, change, continuity, cause, effect, historical evidence and interpretation of evidence. Second-order concepts are those such as society, monarchy and church, which allow us to understand historical situations; and third-order concepts are labels, such as the Middle Ages, used to denote discrete periods in time (2005: 17–18).

Looking at the first-order concepts, there is clear commonality with those concepts needed to both understand and make story. From early childhood, the language of the past is embedded in narrative sequencing through contextualising phrases such as *once upon a time, many years ago* and *in ages past*, and more general temporal language such as *before*, *after* and *then*. Story therefore has a role in developing a sense of chronology. Reflecting on research into children's awareness of time, Hoodless states that 'Stories which make use of time as a device are certainly an excellent stimulus and a good resource for extending children's understanding' (1998: 110).

Similarly, the interrelationships between the forces revealed in the actantial analysis are ultimately concerned with cause and effect. The internal logic of story is a basic grounding in causality – indeed, the appropriateness of different solutions to problems, and possible consequences of actions, can be explored in dialogic forms of storytelling and when and where children tell their own stories (the relationship between story and logico-mathematical thinking is discussed more fully in Chapter 9). The creation of new tales and reinterpretation of established narratives also fosters children's abilities to organise ideas for themselves using higher-order thinking skills such as evaluation (part of what Turner-Bisset refers to as syntactic knowledge). Although Hoodless's research on children's sense of chronology reflected on the role of children's literature rather than oral storytelling, the dialogic nature of shared storytelling enables children to negotiate the structure of the tale, to use the evidence of the narrative as it develops to structure logical conclusions – in other words, to develop the meta-cognitive skills needed to develop historical awareness.

Developing multiple perspectives on historical events

As discussed previously, the use of a meta-analysis of narrative allows us to create a coherent narrative from a particular standpoint – connecting the forces behind a series of events or episodes in relation to their impact on a significant character or group of characters. If, for example, we were to look at the events behind the Norman Conquest of England in 1066, we could choose to tell either the tale of Duke William of Normandy or that of Harold Godwinson (King Harold II). In order to understand events from these opposed standpoints, we need to consider the functions that operate in the historical narrative for each leader. By placing William as the subject, we generate one schema; with Harold as the subject, a contrasting schema is generated (Table 7.2).

Clearly, neither schema provides a sufficient study of the Conquest, and it should be emphasised that children should not be taught to make schematic diagrams of actantial function at Key Stage 2. However, in trying to make sense of the story, this analysis helps us to identify the key elements that create a coherent narrative from the history – take one of these elements away, and the narrative is incomplete and fails to make sense. By telling two contrasting stories, concentrating on narrative teaching, we are simply connecting with the way in which we naturally deal with information.

The actantial schema provides a useful tool for selecting, from a vast field of historical information, those components needed to construct a coherent narrative. Of course, the events to be narrated need to be ordered (introduction, problem, event(s) and resolution) in a way that makes sense of the internal forces and the evaluative stance established (was King Harold II defending Anglo-Saxon liberties, or simply a 'chancer'?). The evaluative stance could also be hinted at in the abstract and coda that 'top and tail' the storytelling.

TABLE 7.2 Schematic questioning: developing a narrative of the Norman Conquest of 1066

ACTANT	QUESTION	WILLIAM	HAROLD
Subject	Who is this story about?	Duke William of Normandy	Harold Godwinson (King Harold II of England)
Object	What do they want to do?	To gain his rightful crown of England	To defend his crown against the Normans
Sender	What makes them want to do this?	The ambition of William and the will of King Edward of England, who had named William as his successor (according to the Norman chroniclers)	The ambition of William and the invading Normans
Receiver	Who will benefit if they succeed?	William and the Norman aristocracy	Harold and the Anglo-Saxons
Opponent	What is working against them?	The terrain (the Normans have to fight uphill) and having to fight on foreign soil	The Anglo-Saxons' indiscipline and exhaustion (they had to travel to the south coast to meet the Normans immediately after defeating an invading Danish army at Stamford Bridge in Yorkshire)
Helper	What is working for them?	The Anglo-Saxons' indiscipline and exhaustion	The terrain (the Anglo-Saxons are defending a hill) and fighting on his native soil

Short tales of tall ships – storytelling the Spanish Armada

To develop this approach to history, we are going to consider how the events that surround the Spanish Armada could be contextualised with storytelling as part of a project on the Tudors.

This period of English history coincided with, and was formed by, the great European religious wars of the Reformation. The popularity of the Tudors as a choice of topic is hardly surprising, given the colourful lives of its main players – and one should not forget that not only do the dynastic trials and tribulations provide memorable stories, but they also form a background to the life and works of William Shakespeare (another rich source for classroom storytelling – see Chapter 12).

The context for this storytelling is, then, a project on the Tudors. The children already have a knowledge of Elizabeth Tudor's perilous journey from beloved child (of Henry VIII's marriage with Anne Boleyn), to illegitimate princess (when her mother was executed), to beloved sister (of the protestant Edward VI), to protestant threat (to her Catholic sister Mary I). By the time of the story of the Armada, she has arrived safely, crowned as the Virgin Queen: Gloriana.

As with the tale of the Norman Conquest, we need to consider whose story we are going to tell. Tales told from the perspective of Elizabeth I, Philip II (King of Spain), or the sailors and the people of England all produce contrasting narratives, and we will consider the first two of these.

Starting with Elizabeth, her object must be to keep her throne and defeat those who would take it from her. The question as to why she should want to do this (sender) is interesting, and not as simple as it at first appears. The problem returns us to the discussion above around the editorial role of the storyteller in selecting particular episodes (or historical forces) to create what is an artificial beginning to a story. References in the introduction to the Protestant Settlement, England's isolation from Catholic Europe (with Philip II of Spain as its pre-eminent monarch), and the subsequent excommunication of the English queen contextualise the story. Elizabeth's opponent, then, is the power of Philip expressed in the invading fleet, the Armada, commanded by the Duke of Parma. In the end, her helpers were too powerful for Philip to succeed: the combination of more nimble English ships, the rapid English cannon fire, the strategic use of fireships and the weather in the Channel overwhelmed the larger Spanish fleet. The winds scattered the Spanish ships and pushed them north so that they had to circumnavigate the coast of Britain, where many of the ships were wrecked. The nature of the story of the Virgin Queen inspiring the sailors of little England to challenge the might of Spain lends itself to an evaluative approach that casts Elizabeth as the hero and Philip as the villain – in which case the receiver of the benefit of the positive outcome are the people and nation of England. The structure of the story is represented as a storyline in Figure 7.4.

A telling of the events of the Armada based on this narrative structure would be unashamedly from the perspective of one side, and one that certainly chimes with the version that I learned as a child. However, it would be easy to see how the child from a Spanish background, or simply from a Roman Catholic home, could easily resent the casting of their cultural inheritance in a villainous role. Although the teacher/ storyteller needs to engage the class emotionally with the struggle that lies at the heart of a tale, the very partiality that creates contrasting characters as heroes and villains from particular viewpoints can aid our understanding of how histories come to be transmitted. Presuming that we started with the story of Elizabeth, we could now work with the children to construct Philip's tale: the same historical events, but a different narrative (Table 7.3).

Starting from these revised actantial relationships, the narrative can be constructed to reflect the standpoint of the Spanish King, with evaluative elements reflecting the rightness of his cause.

Summary

Relationships are of primary importance in the study of both geography and history at Key Stages 1 and 2. In history, we are concerned with the lives of people in the past, how they have affected our present, and how they differ from our own lives; in

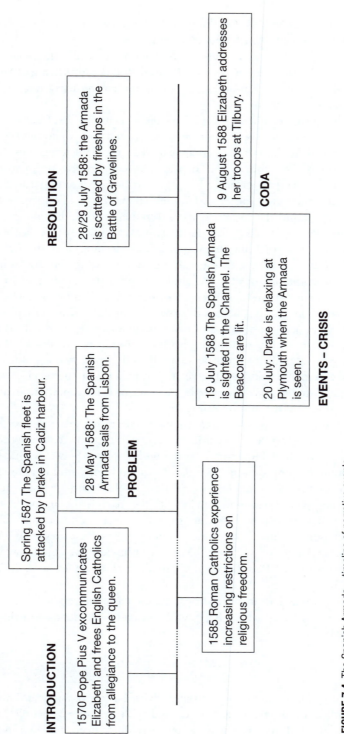

INTRODUCTION

1570 Pope Pius V excommunicates Elizabeth and frees English Catholics from allegiance to the queen.

Spring 1587 The Spanish fleet is attacked by Drake in Cadiz harbour.

PROBLEM

28 May 1588: The Spanish Armada sails from Lisbon.

1585 Roman Catholics experience increasing restrictions on religious freedom.

EVENTS – CRISIS

19 July 1588 The Spanish Armada is sighted in the Channel. The Beacons are lit.

20 July: Drake is relaxing at Plymouth when the Armada is seen.

RESOLUTION

28/29 July 1588: the Armada is scattered by fireships in the Battle of Gravelines.

CODA

9 August 1588 Elizabeth addresses her troops at Tilbury.

FIGURE 7.4 The Spanish Armada – timeline of narrative events

TABLE 7.3 Schematic questioning: developing a narrative of the Spanish Armada of 1588

ACTANT	QUESTION	ELIZABETH	PHILIP
Subject	Who is this story about?	Queen Elizabeth I of England	King Philip II of Spain
Object	What do they want to do?	To preserve her throne	To gain the English throne and restore the Catholic Church in England
Sender	What makes them want to do this?	The Pope's excommunication of Elizabeth and Philip II's grievances again Elizabeth's England	England is ruled by a heretic and its navy interferes with the government and expansion of the Spanish Empire
Receiver	Who will benefit if they succeed?	Elizabeth I and (by extension) England	Philip II, Catholic Europe (and the English people being returned to the Catholic faith)
Opponent	What is working against them?	The power of Philip II as expressed in the Armada	The English navy and the weather
Helper	What is working for them?	The English navy and the weather	The power of Philip II as expressed in the Armada

geography, the study of the physical environment starts with a child's relationship to their own surroundings. The structuring of these relationships can be held in narrative form, which, when told as story, can bring topics to life. There is a danger, however, in the telling of historical narrative in particular, that the storyteller can limit perspectives on events in the past, reducing intricate webs of cause and effect to simple one-dimensional tales. The teacher needs to keep a 'weather eye' on the meta-narrative of historical stories, and to ensure that the complexity is not simplified to the point of bias. Having said that, however, story remains the natural vehicle to give the environment significance and historical events clarity.

Telling valuable tales and exploring deep meaning: Religious education and moral development

From the start of this chapter, it needs to be said that there is no intention here to place religious and moral education on a par. To do so would, at the same time as outraging secularists, who see no need for codes of conduct to have a divine source, irritate many specialists in religious education, who rightly resist the reduction of centuries of religious belief and practice to a means of controlling children's behaviour. The intention is, rather, to highlight the sensitivity needed on approaching stories whose most important components are the values and beliefs that they convey.

There is, naturally, some sense in which every storytelling event is value-laden and reveals our beliefs, values and prejudices: from retelling a parable of Jesus (in which 'right' behaviours and beliefs are played out) to entertaining friends with a risqué joke (the telling of which demonstrates both the values of freedom of speech within friendships and, at the same time, attitudes to sexual mores). Although the latter example is unlikely to be played out in the primary classroom, every time we tell (or indeed read) a story, we are marking out those values that we wish to share. Susan Butcher cites Walter Fisher's *Human Communication as Narration* (1987) as she discusses the value-bound nature of narrative:

> First, the story is a story of values. Second, these values are appropriate for the moral of the story and decisions made by the characters. Third, the value is consistent with one's own experience. Finally, the value/s are part of an ideal vision for human conduct.
>
> (2006: 199)

This final aspect of stories, the revealing of values that are an 'ideal vision for human conduct', provides a stepping stone to the discussion of the use of storytelling in religious education and those sessions in which children engage in moral and ethical discussion (such as personal social and health education, PSHE). As stated above, religious and moral teaching are not going to be equated; however, their common concern with values means that both these areas of education draw on what can be referred to as the 'deep level' of narrative more than those curriculum areas in which the content itself, and the conceptual links between elements of the content, are to the fore. Returning to Greimasian narrative theory (see Chapter 2), we can regard story as existing on four levels: surface, manifestative, narrative and deep. Although the surface level represents a description of story at its simplest and most succinct, the construction of this compact description represents a person's ability to discern coherent meaning from the complex web of linguistic and narrative conventions to which they have been exposed. Consider the following description: 'I know Little Red Riding Hood: it's about a little girl who doesn't listen to her mother as she goes into the forest. She only just escapes from a dangerous wolf who, having first eaten the grandmother and put on her nightclothes, is hiding in the old lady's bed.' This surface-level summary manages to encapsulate the whole of the story in one sentence, summarising manifestative, narrative and deep levels as follows.

- **Level of manifestation** – how the world is represented in the narrative: the main characters of Little Red Riding Hood, the grandmother and the wolf; and the setting of the forest.
- **Narrative level** – the structure of the story, the allocation of characters and forces to certain actantial roles, and how those actants relate to each other (the relationships that we summarise in the actantial schema). This is the scaffold to which the level of manifestation is attached, and on which the story is built. In Little Red Riding Hood, we have a girl threatened by the monster (wolf), which is, in the end, defeated either by the grown man (woodcutter) or the child's own resources (in older traditions of the story).
- **Deep level** – the inner mental world, as opposed to the outer physical world of the level of manifestation (Martin, 1997: 79), sometimes called the 'thematic level'. In this tale, this could be the contrast between the girl's innocence and the lasciviousness of the predatory male (wolf). More simply, it could also be about the fate of little girls who disobey their mothers.

Everyone who tells a story engages in some form of analysis or, at the very least, judgement in order that their performance choices bring about the desired change in their listeners (returning to Goffman's model of performance; see Chapter 1). As they retell their narrative, the storyteller adapts the language that they use, selecting the most suitable for their audience (the manifestative level); they also structure the story, and add emphasis through linguistic and para-linguistic expression. Although in most everyday, and much crafted, storytelling these processes may be subconscious, by raising our awareness of the ways in which narrative works and creates effects in its listeners, we are more able to command the means of expression and, therefore, the message that we convey. If, following a storytelling, the children are able to represent the narrative at the surface level in a way that is recognisable to the storyteller, then the different strata of the narrative will, to some extent, have been successfully addressed.

Through a breadth of communication skills, we create the manifestative representation of the narrative level, and in doing so we reveal our evaluative stance – our judgement on its theme. It must be a general rule of storytelling, therefore, that the teller should be aware of the deep meanings that are embedded within their storytelling, and be able to access this level of narrative for themselves in order to make appropriate choices when planning. This is particularly so with stories that are used as a vehicle for religious beliefs, or a means of discussing ethical issues, for their primary concern is the deep, thematic level.

However, the need to be aware of (if not to control) the deep meaning of a story needs to be balanced with its cultural integrity. This is particularly the case in religious tales, where the storyteller needs to be aware of the significance of the narrative on all levels, and not allow stories that are about humanity's relationship with the divine to be 'hijacked' for the purposes of moral instruction. There are, of course, plenty of examples of religious communities (as well as secular groups that demand commitment to particular mindsets) using story to justify illiberal and bigoted views, but in primary school one hopes that religious tales provide a means of education rather than oppression. A part of that education is the way in which significant stories are treated so that the child's sense of their own faith community is not diminished, at the same time as fostering respect for those who hold contradictory religious positions or live secular lives. Out of such a concern, Jack Zipes prefers to work, when introducing religious concepts such as creation, with the Greek and Roman myths because they 'do not touch directly on the children's lives' (1995: 143). He goes on to say:

> they are related to other myths and religions in the world, and by telling a myth that depicts the origins of the world, I can give the children a sense that many cultures have different gods and unusual versions of how the world began and how people have sinned. I do not want to correct the children's own 'religious' versions. Rather the use of the Greek myths can foster tolerance for other types of religions and customs. Since the Greek and Roman gods are so fantastic and distant, they free the children to contemplate what it means to be divine, what is just and noble, and why there are different explanations for the origins of natural phenomena.

I have to confess to not having been so cautious, having told stories from the major faiths and traditional cultures, but in so doing I have always tried to take the educative stance – this is the story as I have heard and understand it, the original tale is not my story and I cannot tell it as if it is my story. In a sense, therefore, I report on the story, one step removed from it.

Although the deep level of significant stories remains at the core, as stated above, the manifestative and narrative levels need to be respected. When I was teaching in the East End of London, a teacher permitted the pupils to create their own version of the nativity story and perform it in assembly. The climax of this dramatic retelling was the birth, to the Virgin Mary, of a baby gorilla, which the youngsters found highly amusing. The supervising teacher could not understand how such a retelling of the story could be viewed as offensive, after all it is 'only a story' and 'they are only children'. While I have seen nativity plays in which bunny rabbits have hopped to the manger to see the baby Jesus, such visitors are an addition to the level of manifestation that does not touch the major actants of the narrative and therefore does not affect the deep level. In this case, however, the central character of the Christian Messiah (and prophet of Islam) was manifested in an ape, undermining the deep level of the narrative and belittling those for whom it is an essential part of their faith story. The narrative structure remained true to the account in the gospels (or, at least, the folk compilations of the gospel accounts), but the level of manifestation was altered to the point that the deep level (the theme of the incarnation) had been corrupted.

Responsibility for the public presentation of this reinterpretation of the Nativity, of course, lies with the teacher who allowed it to be performed in assembly, rather than the children who simply restructured a narrative with which they were familiar. Observing the way in which her kindergarten children manipulate ideas as they retell traditional tales, Vivian Gussin-Paley observes:

> Who are these people who dare to reinvent mythology? They are the children found in every classroom thinking up plot and dialogue without instruction. And, for the most part, without the teacher's awareness.

> (1990: 4)

We cannot, nor should we, intercept and censor every narrative that children develop in their own spaces and times; however, in the classroom situation there is a responsibility to ensure that those stories which are central to people's sense of identity are given due respect. In addition, religious stories can be regarded as artefacts akin to the Catholic crucifix, Jewish kippah or Hindu statue. Such objects are significant to particular communities, and the way in which they are handled during teaching and learning has potential for either enhancing or undermining respect for the traditions from which they come. In an article on the potential for the misuse of religious artefacts in the classroom, Roger Homan parallels the use of objects of religious significance with visits to holy sites: 'The honouring of sacred space implies that teachers will on occasions refuse access to pupils who want to trespass' (2000: 29). This may mean that, as a metaphorical space in which faith is enacted, there are some stories that we do not encourage children to retell in their own words. Homan continues:

> The contract between faith community and teaching profession settles for respect as the nearest thing to reverence. . . . respect is shown to individuals rather than to objects but it is signified in the manner in which objects are handled.

> (2000: 31)

Taking all that has been said above into account, there are some guiding principles for the use of religious stories.

■ Where possible, refer to sources from the relevant faith community, rather than general readers.

- Choose stories that that help children explore the 'why', rather than simply the 'what' questions.

- Where possible, discuss the retelling of the story with someone who has an active involvement in the relevant community.

- In constructing your telling, try to discern the deep level of the tale (a member of the faith community could help with this), and make a note of the essential elements of the manifestative level that need to be maintained in order to be true to the tradition. Do not divert from the narrative structure of the original tale.

- While maintenance of the deep, manifestative and narrative levels is important, it is possible to engage the children in dialogue so that the storytelling is a communal event. The participation needs to be carefully managed, however, so that the story is discussed, but not changed. If you are intending to use teacher-directed interactive storytelling, check that it would be appropriate to act out the story, and do not ask children to participate unless you are sure that this would not cause offence at home (it would not be appropriate for children to act the role of the Prophet Mohammed or the Sikh Gurus, for instance).

- Do not pretend to be a member of a community to which you do not belong – I have seen a white Briton tell Native American creation stories adopting a 'cod' accent and exaggerated stereotypical gestures. This is not the handling of an artefact that signifies respect to individuals.

Storytelling for moral and ethical development

In Chapter 3 we identified the presence of a 'socially constructive message' as one of the possible criteria by which stories could be selected for classroom use. Storytelling provides a powerful tool to influence young minds, but it is all too easy to forget the messages that are inherent in every tale that we tell, including those stories that are most familiar. Bearing this in mind, we cannot afford to ignore the moral component of the deep level of a narrative, and need to acknowledge the cumulative message of how the narrative represents the world (through the level of manifestation), reflecting, evaluating and challenging social and ethical norms. Jerome Bruner goes to the crux of this issue:

> Stories must necessarily . . . relate to what is morally valued, morally appropriate, or morally uncertain . . . To tell a story is inescapably to take a moral stance, even if it is a moral stance against moral stances.
>
> (1990: 50–51)

The briefest of glances at traditional tales of many cultures (not least the tradition of the European fairy tale) reveals deep assumptions about gender, race and class. The question is whether we see these as instructional texts for the modern age, or a stimulus to generate thought and critique. Although the truth almost certainly lies somewhere between the two, there is an approach that regards traditional stories as having what Joe Winston refers to as a 'quasi-religious universalism' (1998: 36). Such universalism places traditional story alongside cultural myth in significance. Joseph Campbell's ground-breaking work *The Hero with a Thousand Faces* draws common threads from world mythology, identifying them as fundamental expressions of what it means to be human:

> In his life-form the individual is necessarily only a fraction and distortion of the total image of man. He is limited either as male or as female; at any given period of his life he is again limited as child, youth, mature adult, or ancient; furthermore, in his lifetime he is necessarily specialised as craftsman, tradesman, servant, or thief, priest, leader, wife, nun or harlot; he cannot be all.
>
> (1949: 382–383)

For Campbell, myth (and its related ceremonies) links the individual with their society, making the whole visible and present. Placing traditional stories within this conceptual model, they can be regarded as having an integrity by virtue of their origins and development. These stories have a metaphorical significance and, although we have already referred to story as 'mirror' and 'window' in relation to working with minority ethnic children, the story metaphor is presumed to have a universal application: through the window of story, I see the world populated by those who are not me, by those who are everyone else – the 'total image of man' [*sic*]. At the same time, through the mirror of story, I can see I am that 'modest protagonist' (Swann Jones, 2002: 75), the ordinary person around whom extraordinary events can turn.

In contrast to the mythic approach, Bruno Bettelheim employed Freudian psychology to reclaim the European fairy tale as an important influence on the emotional development of the child. He suggest that such stories use symbolism to externalise the problems and anxieties, removing them from the child's world so that they can be viewed from a distance.

> The fairy story, although it may begin with the child's psychological state of mind – such as feelings of rejection when compared to siblings, like Cinderella's – never starts with his physical reality. No child has to sit among the ashes, like Cinderella, or is deliberately deserted in a dense wood, like Hansel and Gretel, because a physical similarity would be too scary to the child, and 'hit too close to home for comfort' when giving comfort is one of the purposes of fairy tales.
>
> (1976: 62)

For Bettleheim, then, to meddle with folk tradition is to undermine tales that have developed over centuries to meet the profound needs of developing minds, and that enable children to negotiate their relationships with their families and those around them. Such a view does not see the stories as grounded in, and relevant to, particular communities at specific times in history, but as having a general application to humanity.

Rejecting both the mythic and Freudian views, a 'revisionist' view is championed by, among others, Jack Zipes (1994, 1995). For Zipes, the fairy tale tradition cannot be separated from the socio-political milieu from which it arose. One only has to look at the tales of the Grimm Brothers to see an embedded feudalism, in which the right of absolute monarchs to command life and death is not challenged; women are often reduced to victims, whose only hope is a male rescuer; age and disfigurement can be signifiers of evil intent; and racial stereotypes serve as useful shorthand. Where Bettelheim sees the working out of children's anxieties, Zipes finds stories that can be deeply damaging to children. Not only are children in such narratives often abused, but the children themselves are viewed as authors of their own abuse:

> [in 'Little Red Riding Hood'] the poor heroine is held accountable for both her own rape and Granny's. Never, she tells everyone at the end of the tale, will she ever veer from the straight path. Children are not to explore nature. They are not to be adventurous. They are to be afraid of the world.
>
> (1995: 221)

For Zipes, when storytellers and teachers use tales such as these, they ignore the fact that these stories 'rationalize the trauma of abuse' (1995: 222). Zipes sees revision as an important aspect of making stories appropriate for children today:

> The purpose of producing a revised fairy tale is to create something new that incorporates the critical and creative thinking of the producer and corresponds to the changed demands and tastes of audiences. As a result of transformed values, the revised classical fairy tale seeks to alter the reader's views of traditional patterns, images and codes.
>
> (1994: 9)

Zipes certainly does not, however, advocate the saccharine sweetness that can characterise the revisions of traditional tales perpetrated by, for example, the Disney corporation, but the presence of the socially constructive message is clearly important to ways of thinking.

An alternative approach to both the 'quasi-religious' and the revisionist is one in which children are able to address the issues that reveal themselves in story through dialogic talk. Winston suggests an

> inclusive perspective which rejects the quasi-religious universalism of Campbell and Bettelheim whilst respecting their sensitivity to the power of the symbolisms and narrative structures of the tales; and which seeks to combine this respect with a critical mistrust of distortedly inappropriate moral values that may have been layered into them.
>
> (1998: 36)

In this way, the teacher/storyteller can use traditional tales as a stimulus to critical discussion on the nature of the narrative leading to value-related learning (such as citizenship studies or PSHE). Of course, the teacher is not a neutral conduit for traditional tales and the values they carry. The evaluative aspect of the storytelling can help to heighten or diminish the inherent statements about society. In my own retellings, I have always used humour to highlight the moment in Snow White when the (male) dwarfs go to work down the mines, leaving (female) Snow White to do the housework – a small point, but the woman's unquestioning acceptance of a domestic role is easily passed over.

As a framework for such talk, Robert Fisher has written extensively about philosophy for children and the use of story in 'communities of enquiry'. Such communities exist, where children are able to 'learn to think for themselves and . . . value the thinking of others' (2006a: 10). Although, in this context, 'thinking stories' can provide a stimulus to enable children to move from the concrete and particular to the abstract and conceptual, it is worth remembering that children are familiar with abstract concepts such as loyalty, love, rejection and betrayal from an early age (Egan, 1986). Of course, such discussion should not be limited only to those times when ethical topics are to the fore, and Fisher advocates forms of questioning that develop higher-order thinking in a variety of contexts. The aim, however, remains to prompt children to engage in purposeful and focused talk, in which they can effectively critique ideas and 'develop the skills and dispositions of active citizenship' (Fisher, 2006a: 19).

One of the questions that regularly occurs after storytelling is 'is that story true?', which is a deeply philosophical enquiry that could lead to a valuable discussion on the nature of truth and the values enshrined in story. Crucial to such an approach is the use of what Robin Alexander (citing work by Nystrand, Gamoran, Kachy and Prendergast) refers to as 'authentic questions'. These are questions:

> for which the teacher has not pre-specified or implied a particular answer. They are contrasted with the much more common 'test' questions in which the teacher retains absolute control over the answers and therefore the direction of the interaction of which individual questions and answers are a part.
>
> (2008: 15)

The use of open questions enables a true dialogue to take place, in which children may develop their ideas of 'right and wrong'. The teacher's role, then, is to facilitate the discussion by formulating questions that actively respond to the children's discussion, and it is the children who provide the starting point for the discussion through their response to the story.

The old man and his grandchildren – a story for thinking

This tale was told during assembly, by our headteacher, when I was newly at secondary school – I have never forgotten it, and learned only in the past ten years that it is one of the lesser-known fairy stories of the Brothers Grimm (see 'The Old Man and his Grandson', *Grimm: The Complete Fairy Tales*, translated by Zipes, 2007: 353–354).

The Brothers Grimm wrote down many famous fairy stories, but here is one of their tales that is not known by many people – perhaps it should be known by more . . .

Once, long ago, in a forest far away, there was a cottage in which there lived a family: a mother and a father; a son and a daughter; and the children's grandfather. The family was poor but happy; and their small cottage was furnished with four beds, a simple table and five chairs, and was kept perfectly clean. At mealtimes the family sat down at the table and ate from five bowls with five spoons. For most poor people living in a forest, spoons and bowls would be made of wood but, on their wedding day, mother and father were given six simple bowls made of china, and a set of six pewter spoons. Over the years, one of the bowls had been broken and a spoon had, somehow, found itself dropped down the well. And so the five bowls and spoons that remained were very precious.

I said that the family was poor but happy. Unfortunately, there was another 'but': yes, they were happy, but mother and father were worrying about grandfather. Grandfather was getting old, and the older he got the harder he found it to control his movements – sometimes this can happen to people as they get older, not to everyone of course, but it did happen to Grandfather – and he found that when he was holding things, his hands would gently shake. So imagine mother and father's horror watching grandfather sitting at the table, eating his soup, his shaking hand rattling the pewter spoon in the simple china bowl.

'Grandfather,' cried father, 'you are rattling your spoon against the bowl. You are sure to break it! Tomorrow, you will have a wooden spoon and a wooden bowl.'

And so, the next day, grandfather ate his soup with a wooden spoon from a wooden bowl, while father, mother and the children ate their food with pewter spoons from simple china bowls.

I don't know if you have ever tried to eat soup with a wooden spoon, but it is not as easy as using a spoon made of metal – it is as if the soup wants to stay on the spoon, it seems to stick to the wood. Which, of course, means that the soup is easier to spill and . . . well, you know what happened . . . grandfather spilt his soup down his shirt and over the table.

'Grandfather,' cried mother, 'you have spilt your soup down your shirt and on the table! Tomorrow, you will have to sit on the floor when you eat.'

And so, the next day, grandfather sat on the floor to eat his soup with a wooden spoon from a wooden bowl, while father, mother and the children ate their food with pewter spoons from simple china bowls.

I don't know if you have ever tried to eat soup from a wooden bowl balanced in your lap while you sit on the floor, but it is not as easy as eating from a simple china bowl while sitting at a table. Well, you know what happened . . . grandfather dropped the bowl. He watched his bowl roll into the fire as he sat in a puddle of warm soup.

'Grandfather,' cried father, 'you have dropped your bowl! It has rolled into the fire and you are sitting in your soup. Tomorrow, you will have to eat outside . . . from the pigs' trough.'

And so, the next day, grandfather went outside and knelt on the ground to eat his soup from the pigs' trough, while father, mother and the children sat at the table inside the cottage, eating their food with pewter spoons from simple china bowls.

And this is how things stayed for the next week, with grandfather eating outside while the rest of the family ate together indoors – and no bowls were broken and no soup was spilt.

At the end of the week, father and mother went off to the market, leaving the children at home with their grandfather. When they returned, late in the afternoon, laden with vegetables and weary with walking, they found their son and daughter busily working. The children had found some wood and some tools and were occupied in making something.

'My dears,' said father. 'You do look busy. What have you been making?'

'A surprise!' said the children, quickly standing in front of their labours.

'A surprise?' asked mother. 'A surprise for whom?'

'It's a present for both of you,' said the children.

'May we know what it is?' asked both parents.

The children whispered together, nodded, smiled and stepped apart to reveal . . . a pigs' trough. 'We have made it for you,' said the children, 'so that you both have somewhere to eat when you grow old.'

Mother and father looked at each other for only a moment before their eyes fell to the ground with shame.

That night, only the pigs ate from the trough outside the door of the cottage. Inside, sitting at the table, were the children, their parents and their grandfather, and all ate their soup with pewter spoons from simple china bowls. And if grandfather's hand shook gently and his spoon rattled against the side of his bowl, it didn't matter, as long as the family could eat together.

The storyboard and actantial schema for this tale are given in Figures 8.1 and 8.2. Although the Grimm Brothers' original is told from the perspective of the old man, in this adaptation the viewpoint is altered to concentrate on the parental role. In the Grimms' version, the old man experiences a change of state as he is reduced to an animal and then restored to the family, but I have chosen to emphasise the change in mental state of the parents. If you consult the Grimms' version, you will also note that I have equalised the role of both parents (in the original, the father is as disgusted as the wife, but it is the woman who is the scold); I have also introduced a sister.

In discussing the tale, the children could follow the format for a 'talking to think' lesson as suggested by Fisher (2006b: 40):

- focusing exercise;
- sharing a stimulus;
- thinking time;
- questioning;
- discussion;
- plenary.

In this model, following a focusing exercise (in which the children are reminded of the rules for talk and engage in a relaxation activity), the story can be told using

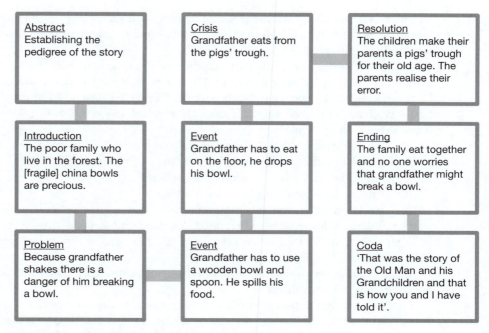

FIGURE 8.1 'The Old Man and his Grandchildren' – storyboard

the same interactive processes as discussed elsewhere. In the thinking time, children discuss the story with a partner and formulate their own questions about what they thought was unusual or interesting about the narrative. The initial discussion needs to acknowledge the children's reactions to the story. When I have used this tale, there has usually been an audible gasp when the old man is told that he must eat from the pigs' trough – this emotional response is a spur to the thinking.

Stimulated by this tale, questions that follow could centre on the issues of the ageing process and respect for the elderly (questions not simply directed by the teacher to the children, but by the children to each other). In the plenary, the children's arguments are summarised (perhaps creating a written or drawn representation) and any need for continuing consideration is established.

This is clearly a 'far cry' from the model of tale as a moral lesson to be heard and obeyed. Donna Eder has explored the use of Navajo and Kenyan storytelling in developing children's ethical awareness at the heart of which is this dialogic approach:

> Open-ended questions and the interpretive approach allow children to bring prior thoughts into the current ethical dialogue. Through the exchange of ideas as well as through introspection, children develop a richer understanding of ethical concerns. In turn, given the rich material they have encountered, children may engage in introspection after the storytelling ends.
>
> (Eder and Holyan, 2010: 23)

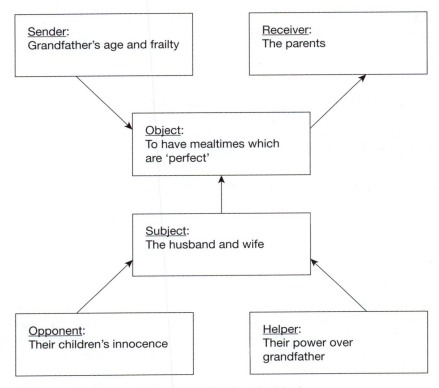

FIGURE 8.2 'The Old Man and his Grandchildren' – actantial schema

The story told becomes the locus around which children can, through meaningful and open dialogue, consider the inherent values of the narrative and the relevance of those values to the world in which they live.

Summary

This chapter has explored both the sensitivity that is required in the handling of significant stories and the potential that they have to stimulate meaningful exploration of issues of belief and action. Tales from the world's faiths need to be accorded respect as religious artefacts, but, handled carefully, they can still be told – engaging children with a dialogic storytelling that does not diminish their core values or remove elements of the content that have cultic significance. With regard to the impact of story on children's moral development, we have seen that all stories, no matter how apparently trivial, have a deep level of meaning. The teacher who wants to engage in storytelling therefore needs not only to have some understanding of the deep level of the tales that they tell, but also be able to explore story and its meanings through investigative questioning with children.

9

Possibility thinking: Storytelling, science and mathematics

The 1999 report *All Our Futures: Creativity, Culture and Education* placed creativity at the heart of both the education system and a healthy and prosperous society. The call for a renewed place for creativity was not restricted to the teaching of arts subjects, but extended to technology, science and mathematics, with the need for 'possibility thinking' seen as a prerequisite for all forms of thought that depend on analogy:

> More opportunities should be given to young people to sense and define problems for themselves, as well as identifying solutions to given problems. More opportunities should be given to the generation of ideas; looking at the world in different ways and playing with different possibilities and alternative solutions. Familiarity with a wide range of problem-solving activities can lead to greater competence in seeing underlying patterns and analogies.
>
> (NACCCE, 1999: 37)

In this chapter, we consider the nature of scientific and mathematical learning, and how story can be used both to contextualise concepts and to generate forms of analogous patterning.

Paradigmatic and narrative thinking – reconciling apparent opposites

Jerome Bruner has suggested that there are two distinct forms of thinking: paradigmatic and narrative. Bruner suggests that paradigmatic (or logico-scientific) thinking is a:

> formal, mathematical system of description and explanation . . . [which] deals in general causes, and in their establishment, and makes use of procedures to assure verifiable reference and to test for empirical truth.
>
> (1986: 12–13)

By contrast, Bruner characterises narrative thinking as that which:

> leads to good stories, gripping drama, believable (though not necessarily 'true') historical accounts. It deals with human or human-like intention and action and the vicissitudes and consequences that mark their course. It strives to put its timeless miracles into the particulars of experience, and to locate the experience in time and place.
>
> (1986: 13)

It is this notion of 'human-like intention' at the heart of narrative that makes its use in the teaching of science and mathematics if not problematic, then, at least, something that needs to be treated with care. By way of example, conflict in the United States over teaching of Darwinian evolution or a Judeo-Christian six-day creation highlights the dangers of creating confusion between paradigmatic and narrative modes of thought. On the other hand, it is not only possible but, it can be argued, also desirable to use narrative as a context within which to explore the paradigmatic. Indeed, Bruner suggests that 'in the end . . . the narrative and the paradigmatic come to live side by side' (1986: 43).

In Chapter 6, story was identified as a key strategy in helping children to use and construct decontextualised language (specifically in relation to the teaching of systematic synthetic phonics). This journey from the concrete and present to the abstract and distant is essential to develop the ability to engage in meaningful scientific and mathematical activity, and accords with a Vygotskian view of child development:

> it is the teaching of decontextualised concepts that enables the facilitation of cognitive growth. If the validity of mathematical knowledge is confused with its origin, or if knowledge is emphasised with experience, then the concepts taught will no longer be decontextualised. For Vygotsky, learning precedes development and so it is by the teaching of decontextualised concepts that the student's cognitive framework comes to life.
>
> (Rowlands et al., 2005: 55)

Developing the ability to separate ideas from experience is a central task in teaching science and mathematics. As already discussed, story is essentially an exercise in decontextualisation (unlike play), and the creation of narrative is dependent on the organisation of concepts. Significant research by O'Neill et al. (2004) suggests that an early childhood ability at creating narrative is a predictor of achievement in mathematics and, although the authors suggest that, while further research needs to be carried out to determine the link between narrative and mathematics, there are links between the construction of narrative and logico-mathematical argument:

> Fundamental . . . are the abilities to handle abstraction, cause and effect reasoning, the ability to follow a causal chain of events or facts, logical reasoning ability, spatial reasoning ability and relational reasoning ability.
>
> (2004: 177)

In other words, the ability to interpret and create story is an essential ingredient in developing children's capacity to handle mathematical (and by extension, scientific) concepts. Results of an earlier storytelling project in Northern Ireland, *Word in Action*, also add weight to this transferability from the narrative to the paradigmatic; Patrick Ryan records responses from teachers, including a maths teacher who asserts that 'The storytelling has contributed to an awareness of the importance of logical thinking. Riddles and conundrums as input for number and algebra was excellent' (1997: 21). Given Bruner's distinction between paradigmatic and narrative modes of thought, this research suggests not only that the paradigmatic has to 'sit alongside' the narrative, but also that the former is dependent on competence in the latter.

Following Livo and Rietz's assertion that story 'is a way of organizing language' (1986: 5), consideration needs to be given to the way in which language is organised in the paradigmatic mode of mathematics and science. The key characteristics of decontextualised language (explanation, distance, etc.) are common to paradigmatic expression and depend on reporting, comparing and contrasting processes; 'possibility thinking' predicts the possible direction of future events and, from comparing accounts and observations, general abstractions are made.

Contextualised language can be used during practical experiments, for example, 'we will attach this red wire to the battery' or 'we take seven cubes away from our pile of ten cubes' – such language is associated to 'us', in this place and at this time. The moment the child steps away from demonstrations in the here and now, they are once more dependent on decontextualised language in order to access descriptions of what happened, describe it for themselves, and draw conclusions from those experiences. The ability to construct meaningful relationships between decontextualised terms is thus central to logico-scientific thinking.

As has already been argued, story provides a model of decontextualised language to which children have a ready access, and one in which they are well practised at creating. By using story, a coherent and familiar world of human agency and emotional intention can be provided to link abstruse scientific phenomena to familiar structures. A story, therefore, can either provide a narrative parallel to the scientific (such as the myth of Orion the Hunter below), or have the scientific understanding embedded within it (as with the Darwinian 'Creation Myth' below).

Story as a context for science and mathematics

An obvious starting point for storytelling for logico-mathematical thinking is with the stories of scientists and mathematicians, and how their lives have affected the world around us. Episodes from the lives of, say, Galileo Galilei, Sir Isaac Newton, Hypatia and Marie Curie make great stories, which can be sourced in the same way as other historical narratives. These biographies could be told with the scientific and mathematical concepts that their protagonists helped to clarify embedded within the narrative, or these could be introduced after the telling. Either way, the story places logico-mathematical abstraction within a context of human struggle and affect.

Although stories that do not have a basis in fact can also provide contexts for logico-mathematical study, there is perhaps an in-built contradiction in using fiction to present something that is clearly intended to represent objective fact. In Salman Rushdie's book *Haroun and the Sea of Stories,* the villainous Khattam-Shud asks the child-hero a searching question:

> Stories make trouble. An Ocean of Stories is an Ocean of Trouble. Answer me this: what's the use of stories that aren't even true?
>
> (1990: 155)

In the context of teaching science and mathematics, our primary concern is in the development of a paradigmatic thinking whose truth is verifiable and universal. However, story is our natural way of representing our world to ourselves – it is what makes the world comprehensible. The American cultural historian Sander Gilman has described science as 'complicated "Just So" stories', explaining the 'why' of the world we see around us.[1] Although we do not want to confuse paradigmatic and narrative modes of thinking, in the story as a context for science and mathematics, the narrative both holds the paradigmatic and highlights it.

In mathematics (and applied science), it is quite common to create exercises in which children have to use logico-mathematical thinking to solve problems that have narrative elements to them. Consider the following problem:

> Gareth goes to watch Leicester play Fulham at Filbert Street. He sets off from home at 2:05 and arrives at Filbert Street at 2:30. How long does it take him to get there?
>
> (www.primaryresources.co.uk)

This method of presenting a problem is far from unusual, and it is important that children are able to see how abstract mathematical concepts are applied in the 'real' world. However, a superficial actantial analysis reveals that, as narrative, this lacks essential ingredients to hold interest. Gareth is obviously the subject, and his object is to travel to Filbert Street – however, there is no problem, helper, sender or receiver. The intention is to engage the child by using football as the context, but the essential elements of how humans relate to the narrative of their lives is missing.

Michael S. Schiro's work (with schoolteacher Doris Lawson) on contextualising mathematics in sustained oral narratives has much in common with the 'Mantle of the Expert' strategy in drama (Heathcote and Bolton, 1995). In both approaches, learning is contextualised through creating an integrated imagined world. Schiro describes the kind of mathematical problem quoted above as 'impotent, painful exercises' (2004: 46) and amplifies this assessment, stating:

> it has been assumed by many educators that the best way of contextualizing mathematics is by locating it in objective reality and by associating it with those things that might arise within children's ordinary everyday life. This assumption is problematic. It is problematic because it cannot be assumed that the objective reality surrounding children directly corresponds to the subjective reality within their minds.
>
> (2004: 63)

By creating overarching 'mathematical myths', in which characters take on sustained quests involving those actantial elements that we have already identified, children can become involved in the imagined world and see the paradigmatic problem-solving as an integrated part of the narrative. Schiro continues:

> Oral stories introduce children to mathematics using children's concepts, thinking, and language and then systematically move children as far as possible towards the adults' conception of professional mathematics.
>
> (2004: 77)

In 'The Egypt Story', children solve ancient Egyptian mathematical problems over eleven sessions – these solutions enable the story's time-travelling protagonists to return to the present (2004: 109–160). This model of creating overarching storylines to contextualise logico-mathematical learning uses the actantial functions of opponent and helper to generate problems, and the corresponding methods to solve them, as part of the subject's quest. Kieran Egan reflects on the contrast between the more 'traditional' approach to teaching and one based on narrative:

> the problem with mathematics from the perspective of so many children is its abstraction from human intentions and emotions. . . . If children can see a particular mathematical computation not simply as a dehumanized skill to be mastered but rather as a particular solution to a particular human hope, intention, fear, or whatever, then we can embed the skill in a context that is meaningful.
>
> (1986: 77)

Storytelling as a stimulus to logico-mathematical thinking

Rather than telling stories in which scientific or mathematics are overtly embedded, there are a wide range of stories that can engage children in narratives that lead towards logico-mathematical content, but do not use it within the tale. The ancient world is a rich source of material: examples could include a story based on the ancient Egyptian architect Imhotep, followed by the making of three-dimensional solids; and the Greek myth of Tantalus has been used by storyteller Sam Cannerozzi to lead into the material properties of the element tantalum.

'Orion the Hunter' – looking at the skies

My first professional work as a storyteller was visiting schools with a touring planetarium from Southampton University. A tour of the constellation of Orion, accompanied by the story of Orion the Hunter, formed the centrepiece of the sessions and provided a context in which to explore concepts as complex as stellar life cycles and cosmic distances.

Norman Davidson reflects on the place of story in the study of astronomy:

> If one is honest, it is very difficult to keep mythology out. The subject is dismissed as superstition today, yet we replace it happily with mythologies about curved space,

civilisations on other planets, black holes, etc., none of which have been experienced. The human being must provide a meaning or content to the universe, otherwise there is a gap left in his thinking. In earlier times the stars were looked at personally and were felt to be active participants in the drama of life. Mythology readily springs out of geocentric astronomy and strengthens the connection with the phenomena.

(1985: 7)

For most city-dwellers, the grand sweep of the Milky Way and the gently rolling carpet of stars in the night sky can be reduced to a few scattered dots of bright light in a fluorescent orange sky. Orion, however, can be seen in the winter sky in the Northern Hemisphere, even in a city – making it a perfect vehicle for enabling children to start developing a 'connection with the phenomena'. This connection can be established by reference to the variety of stellar objects found in the constellation and the mythic shapes created from these objects, whose only relationship in the night sky is created by their alignment when viewed from Earth.

The following (simplified) story of Orion the Hunter is an amalgam from various sources. The aim is to provide a stimulus to the discussion of science, and a similar approach could be taken to any number of traditional tales that explain natural phenomena. For this telling, a diagram (or enhanced photograph) of the constellation could be provided, so that particular features of interest can be highlighted (an illustration of the significant stellar objects of interest in the constellation of Orion is shown in Figure 9.1).

'Orion the Hunter'

When you look at the sky, what do you see? Dots of light? Lanterns illuminating the heavens? Balls of burning gas? When the ancient peoples looked up into the darkness, they saw their mythological world spread out across the sky in a giant, rolling picture book. Each of the constellations, or patterns, that the stars make tells its own story. If you live in, or near, a town, then you will see far fewer stars than those who live in the countryside, away from street lights. But there is one constellation that you will see even in town, early in the winter evenings.

In the times of the ancient Greeks, on the island of Crete, lived Orion, the greatest hunter in the world. Orion's arrows could find the smallest sparrow flying high over the tallest trees; wielding only a club in his hand, he could fight the fiercest beast and bring its skin home. Orion was the strongest of men, the most powerful of fighters, but he had one weakness – his heart. Orion was in love. But not only was he in love, he was in love with a goddess. But not only was he in love with a goddess, he was in love with Artemis, the Goddess of the Hunt. Every time Orion lifted his bow, every time he brought down his club, he offered a little prayer to the great Goddess of the Hunt, and now he wanted to give his heart to her.

How should Orion show his love to his goddess? She was the Goddess of the Hunt and he was the greatest hunter in the world – the one thing that Artemis could not fail to cherish would be the 'spoils of the hunt'. And so, Orion decided

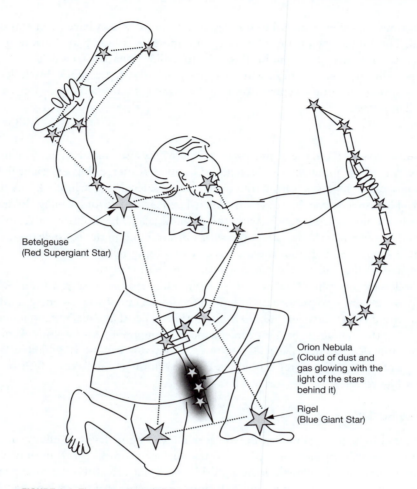

Betelgeuse
(Red Supergiant Star)

Orion Nebula
(Cloud of dust and
gas glowing with the
light of the stars
behind it)

Rigel
(Blue Giant Star)

FIGURE 9.1 The constellation of Orion the Hunter

to hunt. To hunt everything. To hunt every living animal on Crete . . . kill it . . .
skin it. And then he would present the skins to his love, Artemis, Goddess of the
Hunt.

Taking his faithful club, his bow and arrows, Orion travelled Crete taking the
life of every animal, every bird, every crawling thing; he piled their lifeless bodies
in the centre of the island. When there was not one creature left living and breathing
on the island, Orion began the bloody task of removing their skins. Once the skins
were prepared, he carried them all to his goddess love and laid them at the feet of
Artemis.

Artemis, great Goddess of the Hunt, looked down at the skins of every creature
that had once lived on the Island of Crete. An island that once was so full of life,
now was lifeless: no animals, no birds . . . nothing left for the hunt. Artemis lifted
her eyes from the fur, feathers and scales that lay on the ground before her; as she
looked upon Orion, her eyes blazed with anger.

Orion's love for Artemis froze in his heart. As he looked into the goddess's features, love was replaced with fear. He turned from the awful anger of Artemis, and as he started to run, he heard her terrible cry, her screaming across the dead land.

Orion headed for the coast, determined to escape from the island, but as he ran down the beach towards the sea, the waves parted as a monstrous curved tail broke the surface. For a few moments, Orion stood fixed to the soft sand as he watched a giant scorpion crawling from the sea, its tail trembling as it prepared to punish the great hunter for his foolishness. Orion turned once more and ran back inland, trying to escape the giant creature. Artemis watched as her bringer of vengeance scuttled after Orion. On, on, Orion ran; running, running, always fast enough to keep ahead of the scorpion, but never fast enough to escape from it. On, on, Orion ran; running, running until he ran out of land and started to run up into the sky. On, on, Orion ran; up, up he went, with the scorpion following him into his new home in the sky.

And so now you can see Orion up in the night sky forever – look for the three stars in a line (Orion's belt), then you can see at his shoulder a large orange star (Betelgeuse), at the bottom of his tunic a large blue star (Rigel), and hanging from his belt, his sword (Orion's nebula). But you will never see the scorpion (the constellation Scorpio) in the sky at the same time – Orion continues to run from, and keeps half a year ahead of, the monstrous creature. So in the winter, you will remember this tale with the help of the constellation of Orion; in the summer, you will be reminded of it as you watch Scorpio chase across the night sky in pursuit of Orion, who continues to be punished for his foolish bloodlust.

A storyboard for the above version of the Greek myth is provided in Figure 9.2.

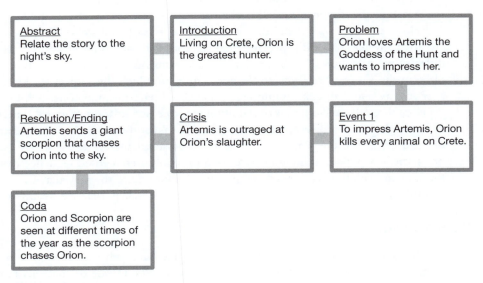

FIGURE 9.2 'Orion the Hunter' – storyboard

To be or not to be – intention, anthropomorphism and story

Some time ago, I was invited to speak to the librarians at Supreme Headquarters Allied Powers Europe (SHAPE) in Mons. NATO's headquarters in Belgium is a community with its own education system and library service, in fact two of each: the international and the American. In our session on storytelling, the librarians from the American library were struggling with finding a meaningful role in an elementary school system at SHAPE, where they were, at that time, forbidden to use any stories in which there was violence, or in which animals talk, 'because they don't'. The first of these pro-scriptions would eliminate half of the world's mythology, the second would eliminate the other half – not to mention other forms of folklore. While issues around violence in story have already been discussed, the second of these prohibitions suggests an extreme, positivist perspective on the world, which ignores the power of anthro-pomorphism to create narrative shorthand for character types and qualities.

From a paradigmatic perspective, it could be argued that using anthropomorphism in stories intended to teach science undermines the abstract nature of the concepts under investigation. However, science teacher Stephen Rowcliffe, writing of an approach to teaching that does anthropomorphise scientific concepts, suggests that 'primary children can accept anthropomorphic formulations, while remaining able to distinguish the factual reasoning behind them' (2004: 122). By constructing narratives in which abstract concepts (such as numbers) or non-sentient entities (such as tectonic plates) can have agency, children can be introduced to logico-mathematical concepts and processes through the language of story. Through such anthropomorphism, concepts and entities are endowed with the language of desire and relationship (e.g. 'the number four *wants* to multiply with the three'; 'the tectonic plates *are fighting* against each other'). This gives the processes in which they are involved a trajectory, such as the solution of an algorithm or an earthquake, respectively. In other words, the paradigmatic is perceived within the narrative.

Below is a version of a tale that I constructed as part of a storytelling set called 'Words to Make a World'. In this group of stories, I contrasted creation myths of different world cultures. I was concerned that a humanist account should also have a place in this set of stories, and so devised a story in which the subject could be the ever-striving life that seeks to improve and evolve. I have imagined one such life that develops through a billion years of evolution and, to ensure that the story has trajectory and struggle, I have projected desire onto that life so that there is an inevitable element of anthropomorphism. It needs to be clearly understood, therefore, that this is a story, not a scientific report, although I have tried to follow a condensed sequence that fits the human evolutionary trail (there are many points along the way that I have not identified). Other processes could clearly be given a parallel 'narrative treatment'.

'The Story of ONE'

This is an old story. A very old story, but people have only told this story for the past hundred or so years. Some people believe that God made the heavens and the Earth, and everything that lives on the Earth, in six days; some people believe that the Earth began as a tiny piece of coral caught in a spider's web, and that men and women were carved from the branch of a tree. But there are also men and women who tell us that the world took a long time to form in space, from the dust of stars. And that human beings did not just arrive on Earth, standing upright on two feet, but started out on their journey of life not as humans at all, but as very simple creatures: tiny, simple, living things – bobbing about in a rich soup that we will call 'the sea'. But what shall we call this creature? Well, over three billion years we could choose lots of different names as this simple creature changes and shifts – we could start with prokaryotes and we could move onto eukaryotes, but we would find ourselves getting very tongue-tied, very quickly. So we will simply call our simple creature ONE, because ONE is the first in our story.

A long time ago, in fact about a billion years ago (I said it was an old story), ONE was struggling, and squeezing, and stretching, and bumping along next to another ONE. And another ONE. And another ONE . . . All the ONEs floating around together, and none of them knowing where they are going. All squeezing and stretching together in a soup-like sea – well, as easy as it is to stretch without arms or legs or fins or tentacles or branches or limbs.

But squeezing and stretching isn't enough and, after 400 million years or so, ONE reaches out – but reaches out with what?

ONE has grown an arm – not an arm like a human arm – not an arm with fingers and joints and bones and muscles – but something like a little shoot bursting from a seed. And ONE is reaching out and finding food, finding that now it doesn't have to just bump and bounce along. Now ONE can use its arm to go this way; now ONE can go that way – ONE can find the food that ONE wants.

But after 100 million years or so, it's not enough, and ONE can feel some of its cells stiffening like bone. ONE is not just a jelly-like ball with an arm, ONE used to bob and bounce, but now it has a backbone that helps it to steer through the soup-like sea. And the backbone makes it stronger than the other ONEs who are still floating round without bones, without anywhere to go. ONE isn't a ONE any more. ONE is Vertebrate.

Vertebrate has a jaw, which means that it can crunch, and bite, and chew on anything smaller and slower – even they also have backbones. But it's not enough and, after another 100 million years or so, Vertebrate grows a tail, and fins, and gills, and Vertebrate can swim, and dart, and dash, and crunch, and eat. And you and I would look at Vertebrate and say, 'I know what that is – it's a fish!' And so Vertebrate is not just Vertebrate anymore – Vertebrate is now also Fish.

Fish can swim, and dart, and dash, and crunch, and eat. But only in the soup-like sea, only with all the other fish, all the other vertebrates, and all the ONEs who have not made it as far as being a fish yet. But it's not enough and, after another 150 million years or so, Fish wants more. And Fish lifts its head out of the soup-like sea and finds . . . air. And Fish crawls out of the soup-like sea onto the land: the sloppy, wet, muddy land. And Fish slides and slips along in the mud – but gills and fins are no good on the sloppy, wet, muddy land, so fins become legs, and gills become lungs, and Fish breathes in the air. So, Fish isn't Fish any more. Fish is now Amphibian.

Amphibian can hop, and walk, and snatch food with its claws, and bite down with its mouth. But, after 40 million years or so, it's not enough, and Amphibian longs to move away from the slop, the wet, and the mud where the land meets the soup-like sea. And Amphibian moves its body off the ground on longer legs and runs and thrashes a tail; it no longer wants the cool of the water, but desires the heat of the Sun. And Amphibian isn't Amphibian anymore. Amphibian is now Lizard.

Lizard can crunch enemies between sharp teeth and run across the land. But, after another 100 million years or so, it's not enough. Lizard doesn't want to have to lie in the sun to keep warm – Lizard wants fur to keep warm; Lizard doesn't want to have to wait for eggs to hatch – Lizard wants to keep its young inside its body until it is safe for them to be born – Lizard wants a family. And so Lizard grows fur and gives birth to its young. And Lizard isn't Lizard anymore. Lizard is Mammal.

Mammal finds its arms are longer to help it climb in the trees, and that the trees give shelter and food, and that its young are safe riding on its back. But it's not enough. Mammal is not just Mammal any more, Mammal lives in families in the trees, and Mammal is also Lemur. But it's not enough, and Lemur wants to be bigger and stronger; Lemur wants to use its brain to think more, and feel more. And so Lemur becomes bigger and stronger, and Lemur thinks more and feels more. And so Lemur isn't Lemur any more. Lemur is Ape.

Ape has a home in the trees and lives in families and uses its brain – and Ape looks at the ground and leads its family to live on the ground, walking along on feet and knuckles. But it's not enough. Ape sheds its fur, and wears the fur of other mammals. It makes tools to build a home, to catch food and to protect its family. And Ape uses its brain to think and feel and, as it is thinking hard, Ape lifts its knuckles from the ground and stands upright. And two hundred thousand years ago, or so, Ape wasn't Ape any more. Ape was Human.

So you and I – we humans – have come out of the sea into the mud, onto the land, into the trees and down to the ground; we have gone from floating to swimming, from sliding to crawling, from ambling to walking to standing upright.

And I think that's enough, just for the moment, or so.

The storyboard and actantial schema for 'The Story of ONE' are provided in Figures 9.3 and 9.4. Note that in this story there is no real crisis, but the transition from ape to human creates a form of climax; the resolution actually comes at the end of the story: 'And I think that's enough' relates directly to the problem ('But it's not enough').

Summary

The relationship between logico-mathematical thinking and narrative is complex. There is a danger that abstract concepts can be so bound to the story context that the all-important element of analogy is lost. However, with careful handling and, above all, sensitivity to the paradigmatic content, story provides a bridge from the

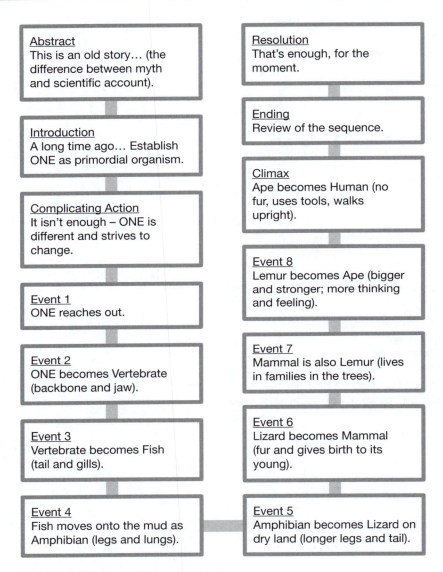

FIGURE 9.3 'The Story of ONE' – storyboard

contextualised language of the 'here and now' to the decontextualised language of paradigmatic thought. Above all, story provides a place in which the underlying patterns of mathematical and scientific processes and possibility thinking can be explored.

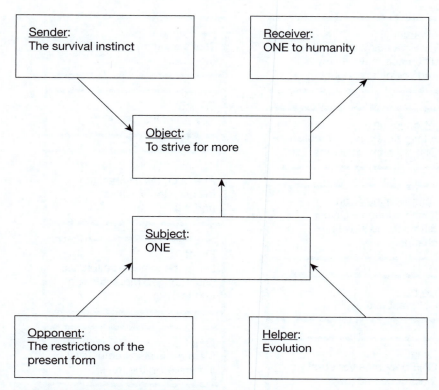

FIGURE 9.4 'The Story of ONE' – actantial schema

10

Storytelling within the arts curriculum

As a preamble to the following chapters on the arts disciplines of visual art, drama, dance and music, in this short chapter we consider the ways in which storytelling can enhance the arts in general across the curriculum and, in turn, be enhanced by them.

The nature of the arts and the place of crafted storytelling

In his discussion of multiple intelligences, Howard Gardner suggests that his own use of language has been too loose when he has referred to 'artistic intelligence'. He states:

> Strictly speaking, there is no artistic intelligence. Rather, intelligences function artistically – or not artistically – to the extent that they exploit certain properties of a relevant symbolic system. When one uses language in an ordinary expository way . . . one is not using the linguistic intelligence in an aesthetic way. If, however, language is used metaphorically, expressively, or in such a way as to call attention to its formal or sound properties, then is being used artistically.
>
> (2006: 79)

Starting from this definition, storytelling itself is clearly an artistic activity, being an occasion for language that is used 'metaphorically, expressively, or in such a way as to call attention to its formal or sound properties'. However, much has been made in this book of the crafted nature of storytelling, and the boundary between art and craft is often blurred. For Gardner, 'craft' has connotations of control of the medium (or artistic domain), and so has qualitative associations that do not preclude an entity being both art and craft. Laurie Britton-Newell defines something as crafted when 'the process of how and why [an object] has been put together has been well considered' (2007), linking craft to Schechner's definition of performance as 'twice performed' or 'restored' behaviour (1985).

As an artistic form of language use, classroom storytelling is, then, also crafted (that is to say that the storyteller has a command of their medium and has been 'well considered'). Further, the storyteller tries to produce something that is both of aesthetic value and a personal means of expression (the problems inherent in this expressive function when a story is historical or religious are explored in Chapters 7 and 8). Storytelling clearly has an affinity, then, with other art forms, and is at the heart of sharing a sense of the aesthetic, the crafted and, above all, the creative.

The report *All Our Futures: Creativity, Culture and Education* defines creative activity as follows:

> First, they always involve thinking or behaving *imaginatively*. Second, overall imaginative activity is *purposeful*: that is, it is directed to achieving an objective. Third, these processes must generate something *original*. Fourth, the outcome must be of *value* in relation to the objective.
>
> (NACCCE, 1999: 30; author's emphasis)

However, the originality of the creative act need not be that associated with great artists and thinkers such as Leonardo da Vinci, The Beatles or William Shakespeare, but rather simply represents moments that are innovative for the person involved – what Anna Craft refers to as 'little c creativity':

> there is a spectrum of novelty or innovation. Thus at one end is something which is novel to the child, but not necessarily to the wider world. At the other are ideas or actions which are novel in the eyes of a wider field. 'Little c creativity' may often involve novelty or innovation for the agent, but not in a wider field.
>
> (2001: 56)

Although storytelling is purposeful and original for individual storytellers, their creativity does, however, need to extend to making the tales they tell of value to the wider group – a model of storytelling as 'social art of language' means that the community of storytellers needs to be involved in the creative process.

Storytelling and the arts – representation and stimulus

Education for the arts is concerned with what the Cambridge Primary Review refers to as its 'complementary dimensions of "appreciation" (knowledge, understanding and disposition) and "performance" (knowledge, understanding and disposition allied with executive skill)' (Alexander, 2010: 267). Storytelling is a useful tool for both developing appreciation and, at the same time, providing a stimulus for engaging with works of art.

The briefest of visits to an art gallery will reveal how story comes out of art – whether it is the tale portrayed in a narrative painting, or the life story of the artist behind it, works of art generate stories. Similarly, a cursory search online for children's storybooks will turn up the tales of Shakespeare's plays or classical ballet. Returning to an earlier theme, it is only natural to use storytelling to make classic works of performance and visual art accessible, when story is how we relate who we are to other people. In order to do this in a crafted way, we need to have sufficient grasp of the elements of narrative and strategies for identifying them in (sometimes complex) works of art. Often works will have a story attached to them (that is to say, a story that was the artist's inspiration) and, in the case of a play, a plot around which words and action have been woven. The role of the storyteller here may, however, be to construct a story that appears to have only tenuous links to the artist's original work, but nonetheless does offer an insight into it.

Figure 10.1 shows the relationship the storyteller has with an artist and their work. Starting with a stimulus which, in the case of much 'classical' art, is often a mythical story (but may simply be a life event), the artist brings their imagination to bear on creating a response (representational or abstract) to that story or event. The storyteller, in turn, uses this work as their stimulus to create a tale that has either narrative or thematic content in common with the artist's work.

In her gallery-based work, the storyteller Xanthe Gresham (www.xanthegresham. co.uk), whose versatility enables her to work in varied arenas, always starts by drawing out children's affective responses to an art work before constructing any narrative. A ready-made story may be found in works that have an overt narrative thread running

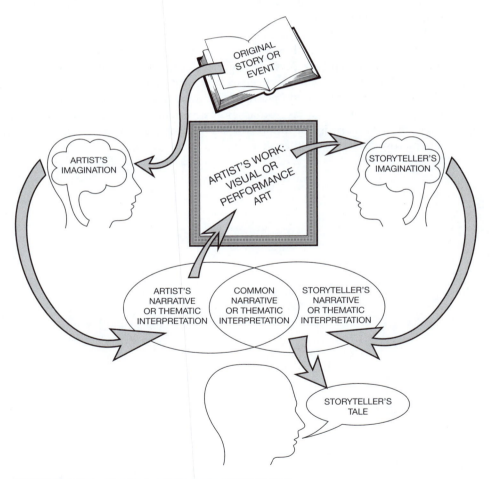

FIGURE 10.1 From stimulus to artistic representation to story

through them but, if not, Gresham links the work to a story, which at first hearing may have no direct relation to the subject, but may evoke a similar emotional response. In this way, story can be seen as a device for amplifying the affective response to a piece of art, enabling a more meaningful response to the work – in other words, building a disposition of engagement. Works that do contain a narrative thread provide information that can be fitted within the established narrative structure (abstract – introduction – problem – event(s) – resolution – coda), story giving flesh to the bones of the artistic representation.

The question 'what do we think the artist is trying to say?' is common when helping children to develop their awareness of art. Equally important, though, is the chance for children to make their own creative responses to different art forms. Of course, such interpretation (particularly of abstract works) may have little in common with the original ideas of the artist. However, through developing an individual response (in our terms, a story), children are making connections and engaging with the symbolic systems of different art forms – a necessary condition of developing both disposition and 'executive skill'.

Working in the other direction, when using storytelling as the stimulus for creating art, we need to understand how the elements of a narrative can generate creative responses, which can be represented in visual art, drama, dance or music. In representational forms of art, activities need to be framed so that children engage in thinking of a higher order than the simple recall and subsequent representation. Rather, they should be encouraged to take on an evaluative stance with regard to the narrative, and create work that is not simply a re-creation of the story in a different medium, but an artistic response to the tale as told.

Storytelling and
the visual arts

In this chapter we examine not only art as a stimulus to storytelling, working with two well-known works of art and a Japanese *netsuke* miniature sculpture, but also the role of story in generating ideas for children's own artistic expression.

Starting with story

When a child makes a drawing or painting in response to a story, it represents their ability (and desire) to recreate a narrative in one of several ways.

- Illustration – a snapshot of the story. For example, in 'The Frog Prince', the moment the frog presents the princess with her golden ball at the lip of the well; in 'The Snake Chief' (a Xhosa variation on the 'Beauty and the Beast' theme), the point when the chief is revealed to be a giant five-headed snake rather than a handsome young man.

- Sequential – a visual representation of the narrative in the form of a storyboard (or equivalent).

- Montage – disparate elements of the narrative represented together without sequencing. For instance, the story of Cinderella might be shown by Cinderella in rags, the fairy godmother, the glass slipper, the clock striking midnight, and Cinderella transformed – all placed randomly on the page.

- Abstract – children respond to the mood or theme of the tale and represent it in colour or form without the image being literally representative of a character, setting or object.

While such activities can be simple visual responses to recall, each of them may reveal elements of higher-order thinking. In order to decide what they will paint or draw, the child has to analyse the narrative and reduce the story (albeit subconsciously) to the familiar narrative actants (subject, object, sender, receiver, opponent and helper). In addition, children can be led, through discussion, to consider the artistic choices that they make in order to take an evaluative stance on the narrative. It is therefore important that such activities are framed in a way that encourages analysis.

To create an illustration (which need not be two-dimensional), key moments in the narrative need to be identified. Preparation for such an activity should concentrate on the role of events in the narrative – is the exercise aimed at representing the most exciting point; the moment the problem becomes apparent (initiating incident); the resolution; or the end? Although children make their own choices, framing the activity with meaningful exploratory talk is important so that they can reflect on their own decisions.

Questions that would enable such reflection to develop include:

- What is the most exciting point in the story? [affective response/evaluation]
- What happened? [recall]
- What made it exciting? [understanding]
- What parts of the story could you put in your illustration to show why this moment is exciting? [analysing, evaluating and creating][1]

The storyboard is an illustrative form, but provides the opportunity to represent the principal events of the narrative in sequence – this can be done by individual children, or by groups working on different parts of the narrative. Again, the child needs to analyse the narrative and take an evaluative stance, in order to make necessary choices about elements in their sequence of illustrations.

Montage enables the child to represent the story in a less literal form than the purely sequential. Although elements of the narrative that have meaning for the child are represented in a non-linear way, their arrangement remains important, revealing their relative importance to the child. Montage may also enable the child to reflect on the story in thematic terms, as well as the narrative – they could create collage using newspaper/magazine images that remind them of the themes they have identified. For example, starting from the ancient Greek story of Prometheus, the theme of fire as a means of sustaining humanity (which serves as the narrative's object) could be explored with images of food prepared on a flame and home-warmed by a hearth.

In order to make meaningful responses to a story, children need to explore its thematic content through talk. It is by developing a sense of what is happening in storytelling 'between the words' that allows children to understand what affects their own evaluative standpoint – in other words, develops their meta-cognitive skills in relation to the told story. Their understanding of the tale, it should be remembered, is a response not simply to language, but also to the para-linguistic elements that the storyteller employs to reflect their own evaluative position. The symbolic nature of colour, light and form explored in children's art finds its equivalents in the vocal and physical interpretation that the storyteller gives their tale, and these, along with the creative use of language, can form the basis for meaningful dialogue. Given this vital role of the performance aspects of storytelling, the telling itself needs to stimulate the children's imaginations sufficiently.

There now follow three examples of ways of working with visual (and plastic) art. The first, concentrating on Matisse's *L'Escargot*, looks at creating story from an abstract image; the second looks at narrative art, based on Yeames's painting *And When Did You*

Last See Your Father?; the final section takes a Japanese *netsuke* figure as a stimulus to looking at world art.

From abstract art to story

Key Stage 1: *L'Escargot* (*The Snail*) by Henri Mattisse (1869–1954)

L'Escargot or *The Snail* (Figure 11.1) is one of Henri Matisse's last works. It was created by Matisse's assistants, working under his instruction, arranging pieces of brightly painted paper in a spiral resembling the shell of a snail.

In her book *How to Talk to Children about Art*, Françoise Barbe-Gall suggests that children between the ages of five and seven are particularly attracted to warm, bright colours and contrasting shapes:

FIGURE 11.1 Henri Matisse: *L'Escargot*

When they see abstract paintings they often link the colours and shapes to actual objects; so a yellow mark will become a sun or moon, while a curvy shape will be a snake or banana . . . it's their way of owning what they see . . . abstract art arouses their curiosity.

(2005: 19)

L'Escargot is an ideal piece for younger children, its bright colours and enticing shapes invite them to fill in the spaces and create their own images of the snail. The following activities provide a model for the investigation, through interactive story-telling, of abstract art (see Figure 11.2).

Step 1: Introduction

The children are going to explore the symbolic system of this abstract piece. Introduce the activities by using large pieces of coloured paper, cut into abstract shapes, to make a variety of images suggested by the children (this could also be done using the interactive whiteboard). If using the whiteboard, detail could be drawn in to concretise the images (eyes and whiskers to a cat, windows and doors to a house).

Step 2: The Snail

Without revealing its title, introduce Matisse's *The Snail* as a collage made in a similar way to the class images made during the introduction (a copy of the work can be viewed at www.tate.co.uk). Discuss the overall shape, asking what the children see, before revealing the title. Discuss the bright colours, and the difference between this snail and other snails that the children may have seen (have an image or model of a snail – or a real snail – to which you can refer).

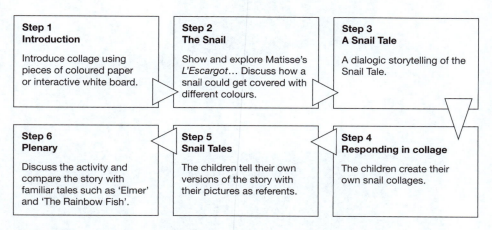

FIGURE 11.2 'A Snail Tale' – session outline

Step 3: 'A Snail Tale'

In this section, the teacher introduces the story, which is later picked up and used in the children's storytelling. The storytelling is dialogic – the framework is provided here, but the language is built by the children as they construct the events.

The subject of the story is Henri Snail. Although he starts his tale the same as the other snails, through a series of events his shell gets covered in bright colours, and this brightly coloured shell helps to save the other snails from the birds that like to eat them. This simple structure means the children can decide for themselves the events that lead to the shell's colour change. These ideas then serve as the helping function in the narrative. The underlying relationships of the story are shown in Figure 11.3; Figure 11.4 represents the narrative sequence, with the children's contribution in determining the events highlighted.

Rather than provide a detailed transcription of 'A Snail Tale', a skeleton is provided below with key questions to inform the dialogic approach.

- **Abstract** – this links the tale to *L'Escargot* by pointing the children to the incongruity of the bright colours in the context of a snail's shell ('This is a story about a snail called Henri who, although he is unusual because of his speed, starts our story with an ordinary dull shell, but by the end of the story will have a beautiful and brightly coloured shell . . .').

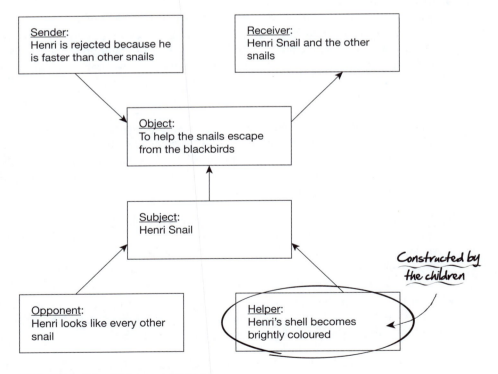

FIGURE 11.3 'A Snail Tale' – actantial schema

119

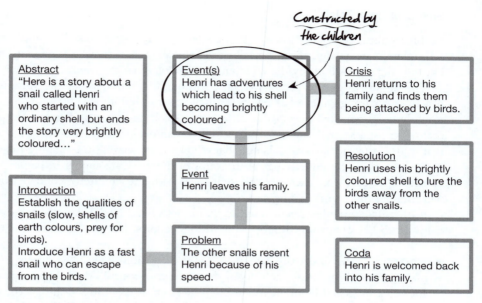

Constructed by
the children

Abstract
"Here is a story about a snail called Henri who started with an ordinary shell, but ends the story very brightly coloured…"

Event(s)
Henri has adventures which lead to his shell becoming brightly coloured.

Crisis
Henri returns to his family and finds them being attacked by birds.

Introduction
Establish the qualities of snails (slow, shells of earth colours, prey for birds).
Introduce Henri as a fast snail who can escape from the birds.

Event
Henri leaves his family.

Resolution
Henri uses his brightly coloured shell to lure the birds away from the other snails.

Problem
The other snails resent Henri because of his speed.

Coda
Henri is welcomed back into his family.

FIGURE 11.4 'A Snail Tale' – storyboard

- **Introduction** – before introducing the context for the story, some ideas for how things can change colour need to be scaffolded so that the children can create the necessary cause–and–effect relationships within the events section of the story. Discussion could include how we can accidentally get different things on ourselves and clothes (a memory such as treading in warm tar on the beach as a child would be a suitable prompt; other possibilities could be leaking pens, or eating spaghetti bolognaise without care).

Once such connections have been made, the context of the story needs to be established. The children need to be aware of the snail's natural habitat, that snails' shells are normally in dull earth colours to help them hide from animals (such as birds) that want to eat them. The slow movement of snails should also be made clear so that Henri's speed is seen as unusual.

- **Problem** – the birds want to eat the snails, and they know where to find them. Although the snails are difficult to see in the garden because of their earth-coloured shells, when the birds find them, they can catch them easily because they are so slow. Henri is the fastest snail on earth and he can escape from the birds – his brothers and sisters resent his speed, and so Henri leaves his family and travels alone.
- **Event(s)** – using the content of the introductory discussion, the children frame the events that lead to Henri having a brightly coloured shell. The image of *L'Escargot* could prompt colours to identify relevant causes.

Once Henri has a brightly coloured shell, the children are taken back to the reason why snails have earth-coloured shells: to help them hide from birds. With his bright colours, the birds can easily see Henri and so they try to catch him – but he is the fastest snail on earth, and escapes.

- **Crisis** – Henri returns to the other snails to find them being attacked by birds.
- **Resolution** – Henri runs to the other snails, the birds see his bright shell and follow him. Henri leads the birds away from the snails.
- **Coda** – Henri is welcomed back by the snails and whenever the birds come looking for food, he leads them away – but Henri always escapes from the birds because he remains the fastest snail on earth.

Step 4: Responding in collage

The children create their own collages of Henri Snail – at this point, the image of Matisse's original *L'Escargot* could be removed from view to enable the children to make their personal responses to the stimulus using a symbolic system of coloured shapes, rather than copy someone else's arrangement of those symbolic elements.

Step 5: Snail Tales

The children tell their own versions of the story using their collages as a stimulus. This could be done as individual, paired or group storytelling; the teacher, or a teaching assistant, can act as the lead storyteller in groups of children with language needs, enabling them to contribute at their own level.

Step 6: Plenary

This step enables the children to reflect on the session and their own collage-making and accompanying storytelling activities. Questions that could be asked to help this reflection process include:

- What do you like about Matisse's picture of the snail? [evaluating]
- What happened in your story to change Henri's shell's colour? Could you explain the different colours on your collage of Henri's shell in your story? [making links between cause and effect]
- If we made another collage for this story, what picture could we make? [analysis of story structure and elements of narrative].

Placing figurative art in a narrative context

Key Stage 2: *And When Did You Last See Your Father?* by William Frederick Yeames (1835–1918)

And When Did You Last See Your Father? (Figure 11.5) is a large-scale work (103 × 251.5 cm) executed in oil on canvas, which is part of the Walker Gallery collection in Liverpool (www.liverpoolmuseums.org.uk/walker). Unlike the Matisse, Yeames's

FIGURE 11.5 W.F. Yeames: *And When Did You Last See Your Father?*

work is clearly narrative in nature: it is a frozen moment in a story from the English Civil War.

Reflecting on behalf of the National Gallery's project 'Out of Art into Literacy', Alison Mawle discusses the potential of narrative art to stimulate children's imaginations, noting that 'It is the concentration of story into a single, accessible image that captures and engages all children, inviting their curiosity, igniting their discussion and, in turn, instilling confidence and passion' (2010). In Yeames's picture, the story is indeed concentrated and, although the picture does not portray violence, or show anything that might be described as action, it is full of tension that draws the viewer in. The moment portrayed is clearly not a high point in the action and, despite being a nineteenth-century work, it would seem to fit a seventeenth-century fashion for historical subjects, described by Diana Newall:

> Representations would not always visualise or emphasise the dénouement, but rather some smaller event that underpinned the greater outcome. Conveying atmosphere, emotion, psychological reactions or melodrama offered more nuanced challenges than just action and violence.
>
> (2008: 94)

This is, then, a form of narrative absence and therefore provides opportunities for children to provide their own interpretations of atmosphere, emotion and psychological reaction. In fact, the scene is domestic, and the time and setting are central to the construction of any narrative. As with the previous activities, the storytelling activity is aimed at developing an appreciation of the art work at the same time as developing the skills of storytelling and a deeper understanding of narrative (the session is plotted in Figure 11.6).

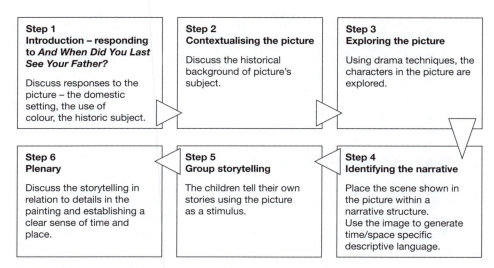

Step 1
Introduction – responding to *And When Did You Last See Your Father?*

Discuss responses to the picture – the domestic setting, the use of colour, the historic subject.

Step 2
Contextualising the picture

Discuss the historical background of picture's subject.

Step 3
Exploring the picture

Using drama techniques, the characters in the picture are explored.

Step 6
Plenary

Discuss the storytelling in relation to details in the painting and establishing a clear sense of time and place.

Step 5
Group storytelling

The children tell their own stories using the picture as a stimulus.

Step 4
Identifying the narrative

Place the scene shown in the picture within a narrative structure. Use the image to generate time/space specific descriptive language.

FIGURE 11.6 *And When Did You Last See Your Father?* – session outline

Step 1: Introduction – responding to *And When Did You Last See Your Father?*

Françoise Barbe-Gall (2005) and Kieran Egan (1986, 1992) both draw attention to the appeal of contrasting characters for children of this age. The identification of heroes and villains in pictures, and binary opposites in stories, allows children to parallel characters with those they observe in television programmes, films and video games. This picture (a story told as if watching through a 'fourth wall') shows a child facing his adult inquisitors, made all the more vulnerable by having to stand on a footstool to face them eye to eye. The line is clearly drawn between those we should pity, and those we should see as oppressors.

Questions that could frame this discussion include:

■ Do you like this picture? What are the things that you like (or dislike)?

■ What are the details that you notice, and what do they say about the picture:

- the costumes and furnishings (historical period and social standing of the characters);

- the use of colour (the boy is dressed in bright blue, which contrasts with everyone else portrayed);

- the use of light (the boy is in a pool of light, while his questioners remain in the shadows);

- the way people are positioned (why are some people sitting down and others standing?);

- where people are looking (who, or what, is at the centre of the picture?)

■ Do you think this picture is like a photograph? What are the differences?

■ You can only see part of one room in this house – what do you think the rest of the house and its grounds look like?

- Do you have a sense of which figures we are supposed to consider bad and which good?
- If this was a scene in a film, what do you think we would have been shown in the scene immediately before it?
- What do you think will happen next?
- What does the picture say to you? (and what do you think the artist is trying to say to us?)

Step 2: Contextualising the picture

Although Yeames didn't base his picture on a particular historical event, it clearly depicts an episode set during the English Civil War (1642–9). Although the scene is generally regarded as representing the search of a Royalist home by Parliamentarian forces, this interpretation is contested – while the soldiers appear to be dressed in typical 'Roundhead' uniforms, this style of dress was, in fact, common to both sides in the war.

The children need to know that the country was split between supporters of King Charles I (who believed in the Divine Right of Kings) and Parliament (who believed that God ruled the country through Parliament). Although referred to as the English Civil War, with King Charles also ruling Ireland, Scotland and Wales (although Ireland and Scotland had their own parliaments) it was inevitable that the other nations of the United Kingdom were drawn into the fight. The war divided families and communities from the top of society to the bottom (often along religious fault-lines) – as the wealthy chose their sides, their servants and other workers often followed them into the conflict.

Step 3: Exploring the picture

There are several drama techniques that would allow children to explore the feelings of the characters in the picture.

- **Freeze-frame (or tableaux, or still-image)** – a group of children recreate the picture in three dimensions, adopting the poses and positions in the painting. An aspect of the freeze-frame that is often overlooked, but is essential in understanding the relationship between different characters, is the aspect of gaze. The children need to observe where the character that they are portraying is looking, and maintain that focal point. The artist chose these very carefully, and they reveal much about the thoughts of the characters.
- **Thought tracking** – when one of the frozen characters is touched on the shoulder, they reveal their thoughts. These can be as simple as one word (e.g. 'scared') or a developed sentence reflecting on their situation.
- **Hot-seating** – one of the characters takes a seat and is interviewed about their situation by members of the group. At the surface level, such activities are dependent on individual responses, but a commitment to a model of social learning means that the whole group can take responsibility in ensuring their success. Questions

suitable for the characters can be modelled by the teacher, and opportunities given for the children to discuss their initial questions. They are expected to verbalise them within the group. Some children in role may feel comfortable with answering in character, but establishing a convention where questioning can be suspended, so that they can temporarily drop out of role to ask for help, may enable them to participate. In these liminoid moments (on the threshold of the drama, but not actually in it), the class can discuss appropriate responses that the character could make. Going back into role, the child answering can make their own from the suggested answers.

Although further drama activities are developed below, it is important to clarify their status. These are drama, rather than storytelling, activities; drama is characterised by behaviour that is 'as if' (as if the character is real, as if the events are happening in that moment), while storytelling reports on events from the outside. However, such exercises can support storytelling skills by helping to develop an understanding of character. By developing sympathies and antagonisms towards different characters, we engage with the evaluative component of storytelling, and this in turn helps us to reflect on the stance of the artist whose work has generated these feelings.

Step 4: Identifying the narrative

As explained above, a work such as *And When Did You Last See Your Father?* illustrates a captured moment in the narrative. What is not clear from the picture is where the picture fits in the narrative sequence.

Of the pictures used in the National Gallery's project 'Out of Art into Literacy', Mawle observes:

> In a significant number of the pictures [the] narrative is not a known narrative, but is simply suggested, offering the viewer a story seed for them to nurture by drawing on the clues in the painting as well as their own memories and imagination. In this way any possible number of narratives can be created from the same painting.
>
> (video transcript, 2010)

In order to construct a coherent narrative, we need to secure the relationships working within the meta-narrative. To do this, we can return to the six actantial questions which can frame a group/class discussion.

- **Who is the story about?** If we follow the narrative scheme of the painting, then the boy needs to be the subject of the narrative – however, the distressed girl (his sister?) is either waiting her turn for questioning or has just been questioned; some pupils may prefer to put her at the centre of the story. Whoever is chosen, however, the picture makes a presupposition of evaluative sympathy for their plight that should be reflected in the storytelling. For the purposes of this discussion, we will assume that, whichever of the children is chosen, the family context is as a Royalist family and the questioners, Parliamentarian.

- **What do they want to do?** They want to conceal the whereabouts of their father.

These first two questions refer directly to information given by the painting (its title and composition). Those that follow require the children to make responses based on an imaginative recreation of the setting.

- **Why do they want to do this?** This question prompts identification of the imagined context of the picture, a context that will determine the trajectory of the narrative. Answers could range from the familial (the children love their father) to the conspiratorial (his discovery could threaten the Royalist cause; he knows the whereabouts of the King; he is needed to lead the Royalist army into battle).

- **If they succeed, whom will it help?** The answer to the previous question will frame the response to this one, but the identification of the receiver will influence the nature of the story. If the answer is principally to serve the Royalist cause, then protecting the father becomes a subordinate theme; if the father's safety is the prime mover of the story, then the conflict between the Royalist household and the Parliamentarian forces simply provides the context.

- **What is working against them?** The picture is dominated by power relationships, against the background of the civilian family being held by the military Parliamentarians. The children are at the centre of the composition, surrounded by adults, and facing a bank of seated men while they have to stand.

- **What is working for them?** As already noted, the picture is full of tension. This is created by the balance between the helping and opposing functions – the helper needs to be credible, but not overwhelming, in order to maintain the tension. Although the absence of a sufficiently powerful helper would result in the children's father being discovered, the helper need not be military. Children could suggest, for instance, that the chief Parliamentary inquisitor is actually a secret Royalist sympathiser, or that the most powerful helper against these opponents is simply the children's determination not to betray their father.

This discussion need not take more than a few minutes, but the key is to engage the children in exploratory talk that establishes the information needed to create a coherent narrative.

Returning to the initial discussion around the setting of the painting (time and place), the children should refer to the picture to support their descriptive language. Looking at light, furnishings, costume, posture and facial expression, the class could create a 'phrase bank', which could be noted on the board, or on a sheet of paper per group of storytellers, or on index cards.

With the internal relationships established and descriptive language scaffolded, the painting needs to be set in the narrative sequence. By providing a blank storyboard structure to which the class can refer, the children can decide whether they see the captured moment of inquisition as the problem at the beginning of the story, its resolution, or one of the events joining the two. The class (or small group) can place the picture within the narrative and make simple notes or drawings as prompts for the storytelling.

Step 5: Group storytelling

The story is ready for telling. This can be done in different ways, depending on the children's verbal confidence and abilities. Whether the telling is individual, paired or group, the techniques of storytelling as a communal activity (as discussed previously) should be emphasised.

Step 6: Plenary

In reflecting on the activities, the class could discuss the following questions:

- Did you include descriptive details from the picture in the different episodes of the story?
- How many different stories were told from this one picture?
- Does telling your story help you to see more in the picture?
- At the beginning of the session, we discussed setting and time – did your stories feel as though they were set in the time of the English Civil War?

Story and world art

The argument about the comparative aesthetic value of world art (including masks and costumes) and what is sometimes characterised as 'high art' (from a Eurocentric worldview) is complex, but is summarised by Isabelle Glorieux-Desouche as a 'peculiarly western preoccupation which tends to separate beauty from technique, originality and innovation from reproduction and creativity from beauty' (2006: 24). The most significant feature of many pieces of world art is that they were usually created for specific purposes (such as for ritual, or to indicate status). Although reproductions and mass-produced objects can be valuable in the classroom, children should understand the distinctions between a work that is significant for the community that made it, and one that is destined, most commonly, for the tourist market. In other words, we should be careful to accord the same respect, and initiate the same level of dialogue, when introducing children to aesthetic artefacts from different cultures.

Storytelling provides an opportunity to place one article of cultural value against another, and to allow each to inform the other. Two of the principal ways in which cultures represent themselves is through their stories and their artefacts; a dialogic form of storytelling (the social art of language) therefore provides a meaningful context in which to explore world art and other cultural artefacts.

Exploratory talk around art and artefacts from other cultures should exemplify the same level of analysis as discussion of 'high art', and should consider the following.

- Origins – referring to relevant maps, but ensuring that tribal cultures are not inappropriately placed within national boundaries.
- How such objects came to be in their place of exhibition – original pieces in museum collections have been accrued in a variety of ways, including as gifts or

through trade or even theft. Objects brought into the classroom will often be made for the tourist trade: copies or items made in the style of original pieces.

■ Materials – surprising materials can sometimes appear in pieces that, at first sight, appear to be traditionally made, such as light bulbs used as eyes in South American carnival masks.

■ Scale – the scale of objects is dependent on their function. Masks are sized to cover the face, while Japanese *netsuke* (sculptured toggles) attach small containers to the belt on a *kimono* or *kosode* (robe), and are therefore only a few centimetres long.

■ Purpose – masks and headdresses are often connected with rituals, while *netsuke* are a decorative form of a practical item of clothing.

■ Representation – masks are often in the form of stylised animals or people, while *netsuke* represent a variety of subjects (images can be found on the internet for use in the classroom, but care should be taken to search prior to the lesson as some *netsuke* are explicitly sexual).

'Urashima Taro' – a Japanese folk tale

Modern *netsuke* toggles are readily available via the internet. These miniature sculptures can provide a concrete link with traditional Japanese culture, through which three-dimensional forms can be explored with purpose. This unit is based on a traditional Japanese folk tale, 'Urashima Taro', versions of which appear in many collections and are also available online.

The themes of 'Urashima Taro' are common in world folklore: the hero travels to the fairy lands or the world of the dead for a few years only to find, on their return, that several hundred years have passed in the human world. Urashima Taro, the fisherman, is tempted away not by fairies, but by the turtle-daughter of the Dragon King of the Eastern Sea – the turtle *netsuke* provides a visual reference for one of the central elements of the tale (Figures 11.7 and 11.8).

FIGURE 11.7 Japanese turtle *netsuke*

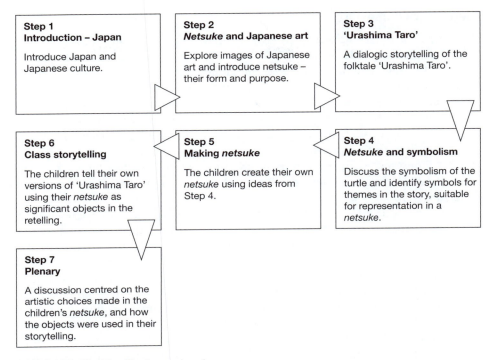

Step 1
Introduction – Japan

Introduce Japan and
Japanese culture.

Step 2
Netsuke and Japanese art

Explore images of Japanese
art and introduce netsuke –
their form and purpose.

Step 3
'Urashima Taro'

A dialogic storytelling of the
folktale 'Urashima Taro'.

Step 6
Class storytelling

The children tell their own
versions of 'Urashima Taro'
using their netsuke as
significant objects in the
retelling.

Step 5
Making netsuke

The children create their own
netsuke using ideas from
Step 4.

Step 4
Netsuke and symbolism

Discuss the symbolism of the
turtle and identify symbols for
themes in the story, suitable
for representation in a
netsuke.

Step 7
Plenary

A discussion centred on the
artistic choices made in the
children's netsuke, and how
the objects were used in their
storytelling.

FIGURE 11.8 'Urashima Taro' – session plan

Step 1: Introduction – Japan

Netsuke figures are culturally specific and have a practical purpose. To contextualise
these miniature works, the children should locate Japan on a world map and be
introduced to some key features of Japanese society. Although this discussion should
reflect modern Japan, it should also include elements of traditional culture, including
costume (the *kimono*'s lack of pockets led to people carrying small boxes tucked into,
or hanging from, the *obi* (traditional belt); the *netsuke* holds the box in place).

Step 2: *Netsuke* and Japanese art

Using images obtained from the internet, *netsuke* can be introduced and the children
engaged in exploratory talk, using questions similar to those above as a framework (it
is worth noting that some children may be familiar with *netsuke* as they often appear
on television programmes such as the BBC's *Antiques Roadshow*). The internet is a rich
source of images of Japanese art that will help to contextualise the story (examples
could include ceramics, Shogun armour, Noh theatre masks, and images such as *The
Great Wave off Kanagawa* by Hokusai). In particular, the comparison can be drawn
between the use of symbolism and stylised figures in much Japanese art, and
representational art of the west.

Step 3: 'Urashima Taro'

A personal retelling can be constructed from any of the many versions of 'Urashima Taro' that are available in print and online; my own is based on versions found in James (1912), Seki (1963), Smith (1992) and Philip (1997), and a storyboard of the narrative is provided in Figure 11.9. In my narrative schema (see Figure 11.10), I have placed the fisherman's desire to be with his family as his central object. Having returned home to find that his three years under sea translate as 300 on land, the box (which releases those 300 years when it is opened) becomes Urashima Taro's helper, allowing him to join his parents in death.

Consistent with the approach advocated throughout this book, the storytelling should be dialogic, enabling children to help in the transformation of narrative structure to told story.

The turtle *netsuke* should be introduced when Urashima Taro first rescues the turtle. By having an exemplar that the children may handle, they encounter, early on, the fineness of miniature sculpture and its three-dimensional form; the cultural context is also concretised, as already noted. As the children look at the *netsuke*, they can also feel the relief of the carving and the warmth of the wood in this crafted item (even if a reproduction); in addition, the holes for the box cord can be pointed out and the object related to its practical purpose. Although this is an interruption of the narrative, it is at one of the points of tension – the group is not going to lose interest in the narrative. The story should not be recommenced until the *netsuke* has been returned and placed prominently. In Chapter 5, guidance is provided on the use of objects and puppets – the *netsuke* is a significant object in the story, and there needs to be consistency in the way it is treated during the process.

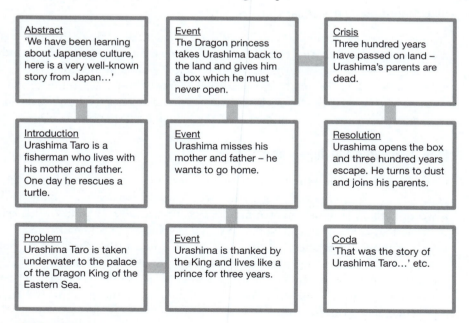

Abstract 'We have been learning about Japanese culture, here is a very well-known story from Japan…'	Event The Dragon princess takes Urashima back to the land and gives him a box which he must never open.	Crisis Three hundred years have passed on land – Urashima's parents are dead.
Introduction Urashima Taro is a fisherman who lives with his mother and father. One day he rescues a turtle.	Event Urashima misses his mother and father – he wants to go home.	Resolution Urashima opens the box and three hundred years escape. He turns to dust and joins his parents.
Problem Urashima Taro is taken underwater to the palace of the Dragon King of the Eastern Sea.	Event Urashima is thanked by the King and lives like a prince for three years.	Coda 'That was the story of Urashima Taro…' etc.

FIGURE 11.9 'Urashima Taro' – storyboard

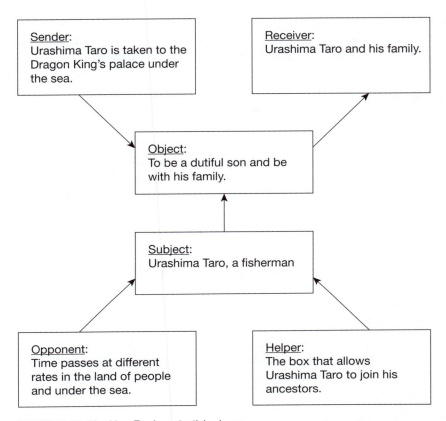

FIGURE 11.10 'Urashima Taro' – actantial schema

Step 4: *Netsuke* and symbolism

In many Asian cultures, the turtle is a symbol of longevity, so it is an obvious choice as a referent in the retelling of this story. In this step, the children explore the idea of creating things that symbolise elements of the story. The use of symbolism is allied to the understanding of metaphor – the symbolic object, or picture, is a substitute for (and condensation of) what at first glance is an unrelated idea – the metaphor serves the same linguistic purpose. A group discussion on the possible symbols that could be created to represent the story will encourage the children to make such connections. While higher-ability children will be more able to identify metaphor (substitution) than those of lower ability (who will tend towards the metonymic – representation and condensation), exploratory talk around the motif of the winds could 'kick-start' the symbolic connections:

- When the winds came out of the box, what pictures did you see in your mind?
- What are the winds?
- What are the qualities of the wind that make it a good choice to 'carry' time?

- If you wanted to show that part of the story, and show the winds, how could you do it (illustration, sculpture, dance, music) and what choice of materials (media) would be most suitable to create that sense of movement?

Step 5: Making *netsuke*

The children take ideas explored in the discussion, and design and fabricate their own *netsuke* figures from modelling clay. Three-dimensional work in the classroom can be size-restricted because of pragmatic concerns over materials and available display space. Because the *netsuke*, by virtue of its function, has to be small, the restrictions in size are related not to the pragmatics of the classroom but to the function of the object. By creating *netsuke* to represent an element of the story of Urashima Taro, the children are engaged in a task that works on several levels, bringing together an understanding of metaphor and symbolism in narrative, with considerations of art and design.

- The *netsuke* has a practical as well as an artistic function (it needs to be aesthetic, but also usable as a toggle).
- The dimensions of the *netsuke* are related to its function – not determined by limits such as availability of materials or display space.
- The making of the *netsuke* is a physical act of symbolising (externalising metaphor and metonymy), enabling children to make connections, not only by the sub-stitution of ideas that they create, but the qualities that they give the ideas in material form. These can then be fed back into verbalisation.

Step 6: Class storytelling

The children tell each other their own version of 'Urashima Taro', using their *netsuke* as a significant object in the story (as modelled by the storyteller). This could be organised as a group storytelling with adult support for those less able linguistically; higher-ability children could tell their stories to other year groups.

Step 7: Plenary

The plenary discussion should be framed by the artistic references that have been established – both Japanese art and the children's own work. Connections should be sought between the way artists use symbolism and that identified by the children as they made their *netsuke* and then used them in storytelling.

Summary

When we examine visual and plastic art, we are immediately drawn into narrative thinking in one form or another. With representational narrative art, the picture (or sculpture) tells part of a story itself, drawing us to create the surrounding narrative. When looking at abstract art, the artist's theme or idea will remind us of narratives in which similar themes are played out.

Storytelling, then, has a natural affinity with visual art, as evidenced by those who use story in leading their tours of art galleries and museums. This relationship can be harnessed in the classroom to enhance children's response to works of art, and in this chapter we have looked at ways not only of engaging with famous art works through story, but also of using story to generate children's own artistic creativity. The role of story in representing who we are also makes it the perfect starting point from which to explore world art. Jerome Bruner's observation that 'story is the coin and currency of culture' (2002: 16) provides a perfect insight into the role that story can play in broadening children's understanding of different cultures and contextualising their own art work.

12

Storytelling, drama and dance: Living the narrative

Drama and dance lend themselves to activities that relate directly to storytelling. Educational drama utilises narrative conventions – problems that have to be resolved by characters, who take on actantial roles in relation to each other. Similarly, when children choreograph educational dance, they often work within a story structure.

However, both of these modes of performance are distinct from storytelling. When narratives are 'acted out', they depend upon 'as if' behaviour, in which participants behave as if they are in the imagined space and the imagined time, and through which they say 'I am someone else, I am somewhere else, I am some-when else'. By contrast, while the storyteller may use 'as if' behaviour to bring a character to life, this dramatic activity is framed by narration that says 'I am me, I am here, I am in the present'.

Although neither drama nor dance needs to start with a story, nor do they need to conform to predetermined narrative structures, we naturally create a narrative as we reflect on events. Working within a narrative frame of intentionality and consequence is to work in the same framework that children use to organise their own lives and learning. Therefore story should not be dismissed simply because it does not provide the freedom that may be present in non-narrative forms.

In this chapter, we look at two approaches to drama: interactive story-making (in which storytelling is blended with improvisational activities), and directed story-making (in which a story is enacted under the direction of the storyteller). The final section considers how story can frame dance activities (using Shaun Tan's *The Arrival* as a stimulus).

The giant turnip: interactive story-making

The Russian folk tale 'The Giant Turnip' is a familiar story at Key Stage 1. It has a simple narrative structure, in which an old man grows a turnip so large that, even with the help of his wife, he cannot pull it from the ground. Various friends come to help the couple (usually in descending size so that the last 'person' to help is a mouse), and the turnip moves from the ground only when help is accepted from everyone. At the end of the story, the workers are rewarded with a meal made from the turnip.

The story's sequential and repetitive nature makes it ideal for moments of absence and completion, in which the children describe the sowing of the seed and its growth, think about the efforts of the farmer and his wife, choose both the helpers and, in the end, the food that rewards them at the banquet.[1] The role of drama in the retelling is to provide 'as if' experiences within these moments of absence. By expanding the narrative, the children's language and communication skills can be enhanced, and opportunities given to develop their creativity.

The principal drama strategy employed here is 'interactive story-making', a term borrowed from Lesley Hendy and Lucy Toon, who describe it as using:

> both dialogue and non-verbal action, which is constructed as the story proceeds. . . . There is no pre-written script and the children do not mime to narration unless such a strategy is used to move the story forward. The role of the adult is to manage and evaluate the dialogue and non-verbal action. In this way, we can take advantage of the greatest learning potential and explore curriculum, emotional and moral matters.
>
> (2001: 112)

The strategy of absence and completion has been proposed as a means of incorporating children's ideas in a narrative, thereby sharing the storytelling competence. In this drama-based unit, both verbal and visual absence come together in activities through which children enter the drama world during periods of narrative absence. The storytelling aspect remains as described throughout this book, with a flexible approach to language. This flexibility means that the teacher is able to respond to the new ideas, fresh problems and alternative solutions generated by the children, and incorporate them into the narrative.

The story of 'The Giant Turnip' allows creation of a narrative framework of a series of drama activities, which explore different aspects of the curriculum. This sequence is summarised in Figure 12.1.

Abstract – setting up the story

The function of the abstract is to whet the children's appetite for the story. A packet of turnip seeds provides an initial significant object that anchors the story to the real world. By having a seed in their hands, the life processes that are central to the drama are contextualised (and the scale of the seed is apparent). The abstract, then, sets up the idea of growth, sowing, farming and small beginnings in the minds of the children. In the absence of the resources to plant the seed for real, after discussion around the planting process, the children can mime planting a seed and carrying out the associated actions (hoeing, planting, covering, watering and labelling).

Once the children have 'planted' their seeds, a real turnip could be shown to the children, further reinforcing the themes of growth and scale (the original tale was told in a culture where everyone knew what a turnip looked and tasted like).

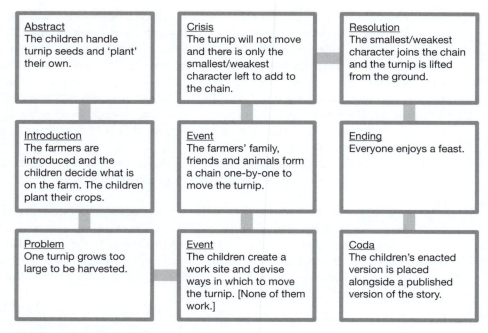

FIGURE 12.1 'The Giant Turnip' – storyboard

Introduction – 'Once upon a time there was an old farming couple'

Through discussion, the children decide who lives on the farm. There is no need to retain the old couple, but whoever the children decide to make their central character(s), this needs to be maintained throughout the process of telling their version of the story. They also need to consider what animals are kept on the farm. This exercise aims to build a mental picture for the children, to which they can refer in their improvisation. It is important at this point to build a hierarchy (smallest to biggest; weakest to strongest) as the evaluative function of the retelling will inevitably centre on cooperation as the way to get things done, and the notion that even the smallest has a role to play.

Having populated the farm, attention can be turned to its crops. In an urban setting, it cannot be assumed that children (or indeed adults) will be able to relate the food that they eat to plants that are grown. Having a supply of real vegetables (corn, potatoes, carrots, beans, cabbages and, of course, turnips) helps to ground the drama in the here and now. Although picture-book versions of the story may provide impressionistic versions of the vegetables, they remove the drama a step further from reality.

The children need to choose which vegetables, in addition to the turnip, they want to plant on the farm. The space can be divided into plots so that each type of vegetable can be grown in its own area (leaving space for the turnip, of course). The aim is to create a single group farm with the children working together, negotiating their roles and developing a shared understanding of the imagined space.

Having planted their seeds, the children need to wait for the turnips to grow. In drama, time is elastic so that the growing cycle of five to eight weeks can be condensed into a few moments. However, it is important that the children gain some sense of the time taken for living processes, and so they could discuss what other jobs the farmers could do on the farm while the turnips are growing.

Problem – an enormous turnip

When the children come to pull the turnips from the ground, the teacher needs to be aware of the risks of children miming efforts such as pulling – the children also need to be aware of the space around them, so that when their turnip is pulled from the ground they don't fall backwards into one another.

Of course, one of the turnips is larger than the others; the teacher could decide to make this their own plant, or choose a child for whom this kind of attention would be beneficial. At this point, the children can play with figurative language: 'a turnip as big as an elephant', 'a turnip mountain' (encouraging them to use complete sentences as the story is amplified by the description). These descriptions could also be noted for use in creating the children's own written accounts, or for display work.

The teacher narrates the problem section of the story: the farmer can't lift the turnip because it is simply too enormous. As this section is told, the children can explore linguistic opposites – developing vocabulary associated with forces:

heavy $\leftrightarrow$ light
push $\leftrightarrow$ pull
strong $\leftrightarrow$ weak
down $\leftrightarrow$ up
big $\leftrightarrow$ small

The language of affect can also be explored here (the farmer is probably not very happy at not being able to lift this giant vegetable), providing opportunities for children to develop their emotional awareness through enacting different states (happy, sad, exhausted, etc.).

Events and crisis – a cunning plan that just won't work

The resolution of the story is clearly the cooperation that leads to the turnip being prised from the ground. However, prior to this moment, the children can devise other ways of lifting the giant vegetable. By treating the vegetable patch as a construction site, children can take on different roles: supervisors, scaffolders, lorry drivers, crane operators, etc. In these roles, the children take on adult responsibilities, engaging in possibility thinking (Craft, 2001) and interpreting the ideas that have been discussed creatively. This is a simple (but limited) application of Dorothy Heathcote's 'Mantle of the Expert' strategy (Heathcote and Bolton, 1995), which utilises children's natural inclinations to take on adult roles and responsibilities in play – as Vygotsky asserts, 'the child always behaves beyond his average age, above his daily behaviour. In play, it as if he were a head taller than himself' (1978: 102).

It may be that it is appropriate to allow the children to succeed in digging up the turnip. In this case, the improvisation can play out with everyone being happy and the farmer sharing his turnip with the workers. However, drama conventions allow participants to replay events, experiment with alternative solutions and experience different outcomes. The scene, then, can be rerun, asking the children to identify what could go wrong to stop them succeeding in pulling the turnip (e.g. the tractor breaks down).

Resolution – a turnip gained

For the resolution, the children act out the pulling of the turnip as the teacher tells it. The text here can be negotiated with the children so that they choose the characters who are called upon to help the farmer (from the largest/strongest to the smallest/weakest).

Ending – a turnip enjoyed

Before having a turnip-based banquet, the children can discuss how food is prepared. By allowing children to smell different herbs and handle vegetables, as well as prepare food in the classroom, the drama can be scaffolded with experience.

Coda

The tale needs to be framed with storytelling, and it is important that the coda returns children to the real world. This can be done as simply as using the suggested formula, 'And that was the tale of "The Giant Turnip", and that was how you and I told it', but it can also lead into a discussion about the different ways in which the story could be told. By sharing a picture-book version of the tale at the end of the process, the children are returned from the drama world as well being able to compare their own solutions with those of the author.

Teacher-directed story-making

Some of the sections of the interactive story-making above were directed by the teacher and were used, in Hendy and Toon's words 'to move the story forward' (2001: 112). Despite hesitations about such an apparently limited form of educational drama, teacher-directed activity can be developed to create sophisticated and sustained story-making. Here, children not only act out the words of the storyteller, but also repeat their character's lines, initially spoken for them by the storyteller. This, then, is a form of scripted drama that does not necessitate participants learning lines and, although the improvisational element is greatly reduced, it does create opportunities for children to engage with classic texts in meaningful (narrative) contexts.

Is teacher-directed story-making a drama or a storytelling activity? At the same time as the teacher–director (or child–director, as this strategy can easily be used in children's storytelling) is engaging in storytelling (as they form the language of the story and sequence the narrative), the participant actors are behaving 'as if ', working in a dramatic mode. A valid criticism could be that this participation is at the lowest level of engagement, creating an active–passive dichotomy between storyteller and actors.

However, with practice, the storytelling can become fluid and reciprocal, the teller adapting their language for those who are enacting the tale, and responding to the quality of the actors' performances.

As the storyteller, the teacher stands outside the drama, looking in on it. Although this contrasts with the established understanding of the drama strategy, teacher-in-role (in which the teacher takes an active part in the drama in the imagined world), it does involve role-taking. The storyteller (or storytelling community) may be omniscient in the narrative world, but the all-knowing teller of the tale remains a role that is part of the overall drama. Reflecting on the pioneering approach of Dorothy Heathcote, Gavin Bolton observes:

> The teacher-in-role's function is that of a dramatist, a dramatist who not only is supplying the words but also the accompanying non-verbal signals . . . As *dramatist* the teacher is dictating at both structural and thematic levels.
>
> (1998: 184)

Bolton's description of the teacher as *dramatist* is helpful here – the teacher in role provides a stimulus to the drama through their words and actions. In the role of storyteller, the directing teacher models words and actions that the children can then use (perhaps imitative, at its best, developed) – in other words, the teacher–director is the dramatist *par excellence*.

The participant–actor in teacher-directed drama becomes the puppet of the story-teller (albeit a puppet that is able to answer back). As puppets, they contextualise the storyteller's language, for those who observe as well as those who participate, providing referents for the characters and actions they undertake (as discussed in reference to the use of objects and puppets in Chapter 5). In this way, they not only broaden their own, but also assist in developing the whole class's experience of language.

This approach is not intended to provide the only, nor even principal, strategy for classroom drama. As Cecily O'Neill has observed, when drama episodes are designed to be 'brief, fragmented, and tightly controlled by the teacher or director, the work is likely to fall short of the kind of generative dramatic encounter available in process drama' (1995: 5). However, the focus of this work is making the narrative accessible and providing a structure within which specific ideas and language can be expressed. It is qualitatively different from more improvisation-based approaches, and serves a very different purpose.

The question 'Why not give the children a script and let them read their parts?' has been asked regularly. There are certainly excellent reasons for children to work with play scripts, and such activities form a valuable part of an overall approach to text-based work, but in directed story-making the participant is held in the narrative by the storyteller as dramatist: the teacher–director is the script. The child reading a script is following (and enacting) the journey of an individual character, and they can find it difficult to step away from their own role – the actors in directed story-making are held in a narrative framework by the storyteller, who ensures the coherence of the relationships between the different characters. In this way, the individual encounters that build the story are held together by one voice, which is able to comment on the way the action is unfolding and respond to performances. Directed story-making is centred on the narrative of itself, the storyteller ensuring that participants are able to follow a story that is coherent and complete; thematic elements and character analysis are more appropriately explored through more child-centred, improvisational approaches. The coherence of the story product is therefore, in some senses, more important than participation – the opposite of most forms of process drama – however, it does provide the child with the opportunity to participate in dramatic activity in the knowledge that success is guaranteed.

It should also be noted that the flexible nature of directed story-making enables the approach to be more inclusive than using a printed text. With the storyteller providing direction for both action and speech, language can be tailored to the individual needs of the participants, enabling complex stories of classic literature to be introduced. In my own storytelling, I have taken this approach with several of Shakespeare's plays – enabling me to alternate between the original language and a simplified, modern text. Children of different language levels are then able to work together, develop their understanding, and experience the differences between seventeenth-century and modern English.

If 'tis done – teacher-directed story-making and Shakespeare

Classic texts can be daunting for teachers in primary school. The Royal Shakespeare Company's report *Stand Up for Shakespeare: Classroom Research* (Irish, 2007) noted that there was concern on the part of primary school teachers about their level of subject knowledge when it came to teaching Shakespeare, and I have certainly faced antipathy to the idea of using Shakespeare's work in the primary school classroom from students training to be English specialists. This section outlines the way in which teacher-directed story-making can be used not only to introduce children to the stories of Shakespeare, but also to place the richness of his language within the narrative context (an approach that is readily adapted to other literary texts).

Dennis Carter suggests that:

> Any school's work on Shakespeare which does not substantially involve children in listening to, reading and speaking Shakespeare's words is more like 'Shakespearian storytime' than a serious attempt to introduce Shakespeare to children.
>
> (2002: 7)

In teacher-directed story-making, the teacher controls the language used, and can both celebrate and contextualise Shakespeare's language as the storytelling progresses. What is more, this control allows the teacher to edit the work and create a telling that is manageable and tailored to the needs of their children. It takes in excess of two-and-a-half hours to perform *Macbeth* as a play; an interactive (directed) storytelling of the essential narrative can be told in under an hour (or even in short sections). Obviously this is no substitute for attending a good staged version of the play, but it does bring the work to life in the classroom and provide an opportunity for children to perform Shakespeare's text in a setting that is immediate and comprehensible.

Such a sustained piece of storytelling naturally involves an amount of preparation and memorisation that would be unrealistic for most class teachers, who are hard-pressed for time. However, the techniques can be employed in telling short sections that, although needing some preparation, require only the narrative structure to be memorised, rather than large 'chunks' of the play (a similar approach is advocated by Carter, 2002). Specific scenes can be selected that are essential to understanding the plot; these then provide a context within which edited sections of Shakespeare's language can be expressed, comprehended and enjoyed.

Macbeth Act I Scene 2

What follows is the method applied to Act I Scene 2 of *Macbeth*. The first step is creating a storyboard that is manageable and yet still conveys a coherent narrative identifying the essential actants (a suggested storyboard for *Macbeth* is given in Figure 12.2). In this scene, the subject is King Duncan and, at this point of the play, it is important to emphasise Macbeth's positive role as one of the King's helpers in the face of the Norwegian invaders and the traitorous Thane of Cawdor (as shown in Figure 12.3). As previously stated, it is not intended that teacher-directed story-making is the only method for working with the text, and other techniques can be employed throughout the story – the opening scene between the witches can, for instance, be treated as a whole-class poetry performance.

Editing a classic text can be a time-consuming task, but the scripts of Leon Garfield's *Animated Tales* versions of several of Shakespeare's plays (Shakespeare, 1992) are available second-hand through the internet, and provide a sound textual basis on which to build the storytelling.

Garfield's version of this scene provides a paragraph of background before going into the King's speech. The information in this narration could easily be summarised, or expanded upon, by the teacher–director before leading into Duncan's speech on the nature of trust. The teacher can hold a script and use it as and when they wish, weaving their own third-person narrative around the words of the characters. When they want to use Shakespeare's text, the storyteller prompts the participant-Duncan with the required words. In my own adaptation, following an introductory sentence, I use two prompt cards, which can either be relayed orally to the participants or handed to them as very short scripts to read. Although this may appear to contradict my earlier position on the use of printed texts, in this case the texts are pronouncements that simply move the plot along, rather than being a means of establishing relationships between the characters.

The characters in this scene are: King Duncan (sitting on a throne), a wounded sergeant, and Lord Ross. The scene is introduced: 'King Duncan is waiting for news from the battle, when a wounded soldier is brought before him.'

The wounded sergeant comes forward and speaks either the original text or a simpler, modern version (Table 12.1).

The story of the scene is told in only a few minutes, with children speaking and listening to Shakespeare's language in context. Carter's disparaging notion of a 'Shakespearean storytime' is turned into a valuable learning experience.

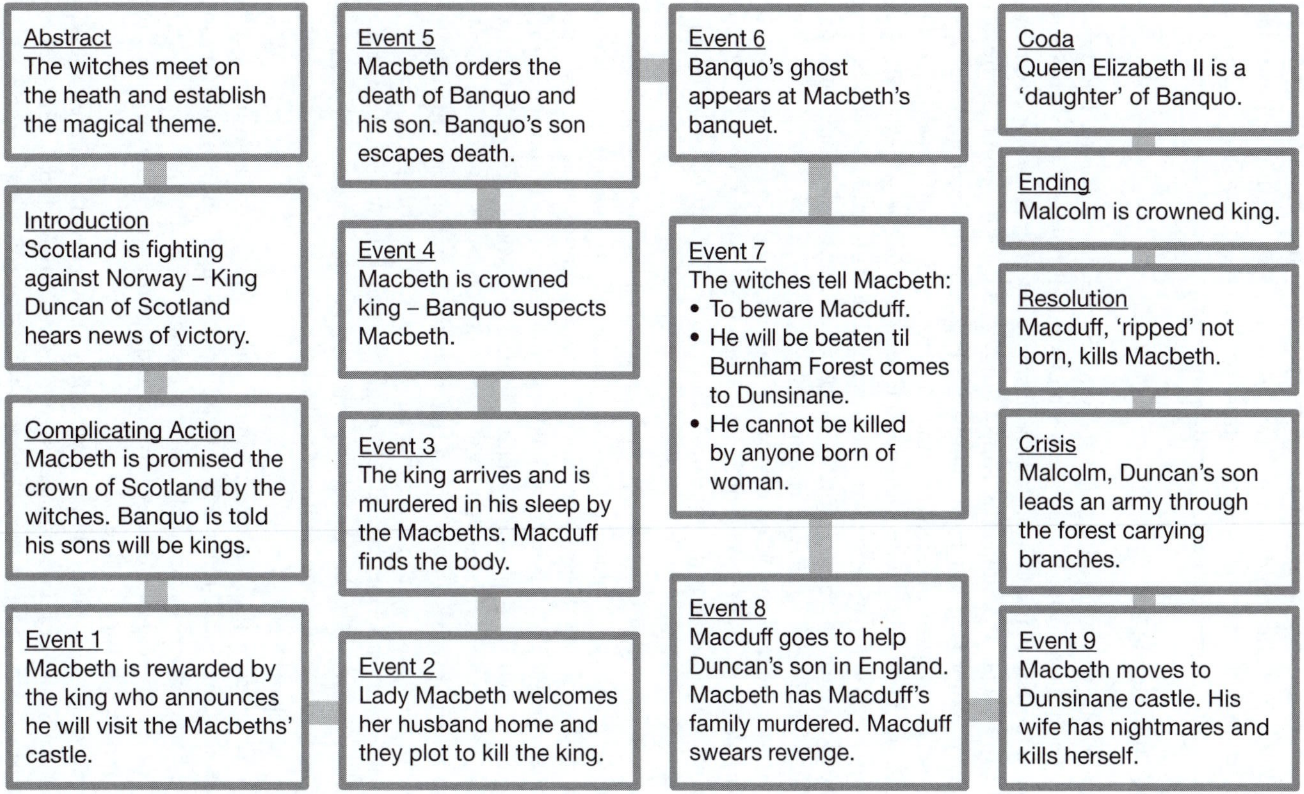

Abstract
The witches meet on the heath and establish the magical theme.

Introduction
Scotland is fighting against Norway – King Duncan of Scotland hears news of victory.

Complicating Action
Macbeth is promised the crown of Scotland by the witches. Banquo is told his sons will be kings.

Event 1
Macbeth is rewarded by the king who announces he will visit the Macbeths' castle.

Event 5
Macbeth orders the death of Banquo and his son. Banquo's son escapes death.

Event 4
Macbeth is crowned king – Banquo suspects Macbeth.

Event 3
The king arrives and is murdered in his sleep by the Macbeths. Macduff finds the body.

Event 2
Lady Macbeth welcomes her husband home and they plot to kill the king.

Event 6
Banquo's ghost appears at Macbeth's banquet.

Event 7
The witches tell Macbeth:
- To beware Macduff.
- He will be beaten til Burnham Forest comes to Dunsinane.
- He cannot be killed by anyone born of woman.

Event 8
Macduff goes to help Duncan's son in England. Macbeth has Macduff's family murdered. Macduff swears revenge.

Coda
Queen Elizabeth II is a 'daughter' of Banquo.

Ending
Malcolm is crowned king.

Resolution
Macduff, 'ripped' not born, kills Macbeth.

Crisis
Malcolm, Duncan's son leads an army through the forest carrying branches.

Event 9
Macbeth moves to Dunsinane castle. His wife has nightmares and kills herself.

FIGURE 12.2 *Macbeth* – storyboard

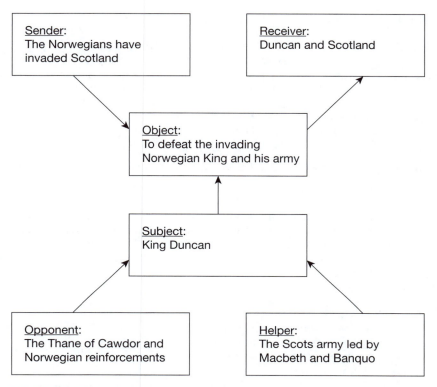

FIGURE 12.3 *Macbeth* Act 1 Scene 1 – actantial schema

TABLE 12.1 *Macbeth* Act I Scene 2

SPEAKER	SHAKESPEARE'S ORIGINAL	MODERN ENGLISH
Sergeant	Doubtful it stood but brave Macbeth disdaining fortune, with his brandished steel, which smoked with bloody execution, carved out his passage. The Norweyan lord surveying vantage With furbished arms and new supplies of men Began a fresh assault.	The battle was in the balance – but brave Macbeth cut his way forward with blood dripping from his sword. The Norwegian King saw his chance and began a fresh attack . . .

The King asks the sergeant whether Macbeth and Banquo were frightened by the arrival of this new assault.

TABLE 12.1 *Continued*

SPEAKER	SHAKESPEARE'S ORIGINAL	MODERN ENGLISH
Sergeant	Yes; as sparrows eagles, or the hare the lion. If I say sooth, I must report they doubly redoubled strokes upon the foe as if they meant to bathe in reeking wounds.	Only if an eagle is scared by a sparrow, or a lion by a hare. They fought twice as hard as if they wanted to swim in blood.

The sergeant is taken away so that his wounds can be tended. Lord Ross enters.

Lord Ross	God save the King!	God save the King!
	Norway himself, with terrible numbers, assisted by that most disloyal traitor, the Thane of Cawdor, began a dismal conflict, Till that Bellona's bridegroom, Confronted him with self-comparisons, point against point rebellious, arm 'gainst arm. Curbing his lavish spirit: and, to conclude the victory fell on us.	The King of Norway launched an attack with the help of that traitor, the Thane of Cawdor. But they met their match in Macbeth – in short, we won the battle!

The King is delighted but saddened to hear of the Thane of Cawdor's treachery.

King	There's no art to find the mind's Duncan construction in the face. He was a gentleman in whom I placed an absolute trust. Go pronounce his present death, and with his former title greet Macbeth. What he hath lost, noble Macbeth hath won.	

(Garfield, 1992: 11)

Children as storyteller–directors

Teacher-directed story-making is central to the practice of Vivian Gussin Paley in her pioneering work with pre-school children. Rather than using classic texts, she listens to and notes children's natural storytelling as they play (which may be based on traditional stories that they have been told). Paley then reads her transcript of the children's stories, and children enact the story as she reads, negotiating both the transcript and the roles as they perform (Paley, 1990, 2001).

Of course, children can also act as storyteller-directors and create their own stories for their peers to act out – a process that is simply an extension of the ways in which children negotiate role in their imaginative play together. This is the basis of the tellings at the storytelling club at Ravenstone Primary School in south London. Ty van Brown and Matthew Friday, class teachers who run the after-school club, model the process for the children, who then tell their own stories which they have prepared during the week, directing their peers as they tell (Figure 12.4). The performances here are not rehearsed in any way. The children are creating story in the moment, they are spontaneous, imperfect and occasions of genuine exchange.

Story into movement

At the time of writing, dance falls within physical education in the National Curriculum for England and Wales, and although its position could alter with revisions of the curriculum (for instance, placing it within a stream of expressive arts), its nature as crafted physical expression will not. Dance represents the meeting of physical training with affective expression. In this section, we see how storytelling can exploit the expressive potential of dance as an art form, and at the same time contextualise dance skills, using Shaun Tan's graphic novel *The Arrival* (2007).

FIGURE 12.4 The storytelling club – Ravenstone Primary School

Dancing *The Arrival*

At the centre of *The Arrival* is a refugee forced to leave his family and homeland behind because of a dark, unknown threat (Figure 12.5). As he travels to a strange land, the refugee experiences the trauma of separation from those he loves, and the strangeness of a new land, before finding work, making new friends and finally being reunited with his family. The tale is told through stylised drawings, but without any decodable text (there is form writing visible within the pictures, but it is as foreign to the reader as to the refugee who finds himself isolated by his surroundings). Without text to tie the narrative to a specific meaning, the book is open to the kind of interpretive processes outlined above for working with visual art, each picture representing a frozen moment in the story. Writing about using *The Arrival* as a stimulus for Key Stage 3 drama, Gethin Jones suggests that:

FIGURE 12.5 Illustration from *The Arrival* by Shaun Tan (2007)

Through the absence of text, wordless picture story books can provide children with . . . 'gaps' to fill. While the images remain real enough to provide detail and ground students' thinking, the absence of text can provide students with a certain amount of interpretive freedom that can ensure that no two actors [*in our terms, dancers*] give identical performances.

(2010: 3)

The difference between the illustrations in *The Arrival* and the art works identified in Chapter 11 is the narrative thread that runs through the book – each picture relating to those either side of it, in the same way as a visual storyboard. In this context, the storyteller holds the overall narrative together, as the children use movement to explore episodes in the story.

The session outlined here is a section from a more developed dance project based on *The Arrival*, which aims to develop children's understanding and skills in the dance actions of gesturing, travelling, jumping, turning and stepping. The narrative of *The Arrival* frames the creative aspects of the learning and provides a stimulus for choreography. The session is outlined in Figure 12.6.

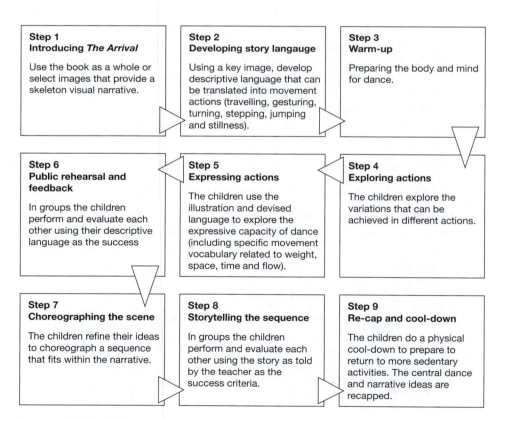

Step 1
Introducing *The Arrival*

Use the book as a whole or select images that provide a skeleton visual narrative.

Step 2
Developing story langauge

Using a key image, develop descriptive language that can be translated into movement actions (travelling, gesturing, turning, stepping, jumping and stillness).

Step 3
Warm-up

Preparing the body and mind for dance.

Step 6
Public rehearsal and feedback

In groups the children perform and evaluate each other using their descriptive language as the success

Step 5
Expressing actions

The children use the illustration and devised language to explore the expressive capacity of dance (including specific movement vocabulary related to weight, space, time and flow).

Step 4
Exploring actions

The children explore the variations that can be achieved in different actions.

Step 7
Choreographing the scene

The children refine their ideas to choreograph a sequence that fits within the narrative.

Step 8
Storytelling the sequence

In groups the children perform and evaluate each other using the story as told by the teacher as the success criteria.

Step 9
Re-cap and cool-down

The children do a physical cool-down to prepare to return to more sedentary activities. The central dance and narrative ideas are recapped.

FIGURE 12.6 *The Arrival* – session outline

Step 1: Introducing *The Arrival*

Prior to physical dance activities, the linguistic aspects of the storytelling need to be developed and the visual narrative interpreted. There are two possible routes to creating the narrative: work with the whole book, creating a shared storytelling; or choose a few images that can frame the narrative.

Whichever route is preferred, the derived narrative needs to have both internal and structural integrity. If the whole book is being used, then the structure is preset (although there will have to be some form of selection process to decide which illustrations to use as a stimulus for dance work). If, on the other hand, only a pre-selected group of images is to be used, the selection needs to encapsulate the narrative thread. A simplification of the narrative is represented in Figure 12.7; images should be chosen that relate to the key moments identified and that lend themselves to interpretation through dance.

Step 2: Developing story language

The group generates descriptive terms that can be used to tell the story, and that can be linked to the qualities of dance actions.

The image in Figure 12.5 shows the protagonist leaving his home and family to seek a new life. His family walks along a deserted street, with a monstrous and unidentified shadow looming over the terraced houses.

This snapshot represents one of the events of the story (the protagonist's journey) which would fall within the actantial category of helper – he is able to travel (there would be many unable to do so). Discussing the picture, the children create linguistic references to the image, which can be translated into movement. From this image, the idea of travelling can be explored, concentrating on the family and their movement

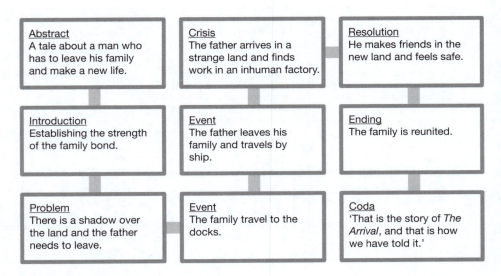

FIGURE 12.7 *The Arrival* – storyboard

through space, under the shadow (*moving cautiously, edging, silent, always looking round*). Although the bigger picture is important (the language generated will be incorporated into the storytelling), the language does need to concentrate on this idea. The descriptions should be committed to paper so that they can be drawn upon during the storytelling – if large sheets of paper, or a roll of lining paper, are used, it can be laid across the floor to provide visual cues.

Returning to the image, the first question to arise is, 'What is the shadow?' Although we are concerned with the family, and telling the story of the father, the shadow is the dominating feature of the picture; any language that we associate with the family is in relation to this narrative element. A discussion about the reasons why people leave their homes to become refugees can lead into regarding the tentacles as symbols in art (which can be linked to metaphor in language). The unnamed threat could be *overshadowing, reaching, stretching, looming* – terms that can lead to the family's reaction to it: *fearful, hiding, hurrying, cowering*. In the picture, the family is simply walking, but we are going to extend this action and interpret it in dance, and so the accompanying word-picture building for the family should not simply be restricted to the literal interpretation of the illustration.

Steps 3 and 4: Warm-up/Exploring actions

As mentioned above, the skills and understanding of dance need to be balanced with the expressive capacity of dance as an art form. The children should not, therefore, be expected to begin responding physically to the text without having the chance to develop their movement vocabulary. Following a physical warm-up, the group should try different forms of locomotor movement, such as walking, gliding, sliding, crawling, hopping, rolling and turning; they should also use different levels (including the floor) and experiment with following *direct* (shortest possible distance) and *flexible* (meandering) paths. This approach is derived from the pioneering work of Rudolf Laban (1950), and should also include experimentation with aspects of magnitude (size of steps, etc.), speed, and alternation between *sudden* and *sustained* movements. These do not have to be individual activities – pupils can work in twos or threes, matching or mirroring each other's movements, or moving while connected together.

Music will clearly help determine the mood and pace of any movement. As we enter into the physically expressive part of the activities, we need to work with music that fits within the narrative schema and supports children in their dance interpretation. Film scores provide a rich seam of music that is written to evoke particular moods attached to visual images, and I have often drawn on Michael Nyman's minimalist music when working with young people. For this section of *The Arrival* I have used Nyman's 'Wheelbarrow Walk', from the Peter Greenaway film *Drowning by Numbers*. This combines a driving rhythm in the strings for the family, with heavy brass overlaid for the shadow (this track, along with other Nyman music suitable for dance lessons, is on the album *Essential Michael Nyman Band*, 1992). Whatever music is chosen, it is important that it maintains a degree of predictability in rhythm and pace, avoiding sudden change, so that the children can concentrate on matching their movement to the overall story themes, rather than an internal narrative of the music.

Step 5: Expressing actions

Turning to the list of descriptive language created in Step 2, the qualities of movement are now related to the description of the family's feelings, and explored by the children working in small groups. Specific movement vocabulary should be used by the teacher in supporting this activity to develop connections between the qualities of movement and the effects they have. Concentrating on travelling provides an opportunity to explore space through *flexible* and *direct* movements – however, the children can also be encouraged to think about time as well as space by creating contrasts between *sudden* and *sustained* locomotor movements.

Step 6: Public rehearsal and feedback

The children can be given a time limit to choreograph a sequence of three contrasting ways of moving around the room that express something of the language chosen for the storytelling. When the time comes for the children to show their dance (one half of the class to the other, making the process manageable), time for reflection needs to be incorporated into the planning, and discussion of the sequence is based round two threads:

- the language of the story and how well it is expressed in movement;
- the movement itself – contrasting locomotor movements that use *direct* and *flexible* paths, and have sections that are observably either *sudden* and *sustained*.

Step 7: Choreographing the scene

Using the ideas they have already explored, and refining them based on the feedback, the children can now choreograph their final sequences. These sequences need to be framed by still images (or freeze-frames) where they hold the walking position of the family, as shown in the original image. When the movement begins, they start walking then go into their sequence, finally returning to their original frozen poses.

Step 8: Storytelling the sequence

For performance of the sequence, the class can be split into groups, enabling students to reflect on their own dance in relating it to the work of others.

The role of the teacher is to integrate the story with the dance. The teacher tells the relevant section of the story, drawing on the descriptive language developed in Step 2. Although the simplest approach to the narration is to introduce the dance with the story, a combination of dance and narration is a more integrated approach. In this way, the teacher talks over the dance, not only allowing the children to respond to the language, but also allowing the language to respond to their movement – reinforcing the notion of the community of storytellers through a dialogue between the verbal and the physical.

Step 9: Recap and cool-down

It is important for children to understand that the body needs both to be prepared for physical activity and to be given an opportunity to cool down after the session.

During the plenary following the activities, the links between the movement and the narrative are recapped, reflecting how characters are given emotional worlds in story, and how those emotions change as events in narrative unfold.

Summary

Although drama and dance provide the means by which children can enter narratives, take on roles and give expression to the emotional states of characters, the distinction between the 'as if' behaviour of dramatic art and the third-person narrative frame of storytelling needs to be maintained. A story can be 'told' through dance and drama, but this 'telling' is qualitatively different from that of the storyteller's verbal art. The storyteller (or storytelling community) holds onto the entire narrative and evaluates it from the outside; the actor/dancer has a single perspective through the eyes of the role that they inhabit. Storytelling, however, can provide a context within which drama and dance are used to explore aspects of the told narrative. In turn, this enacted exploration of narrative can enrich the language of story, as children verbalise what they have discovered through their 'as if' behaviour, and bring it to their own story-telling.

13

Singing the narrative: Storytelling and music

Music has been an integral part of storytelling throughout history, from the *oriori* lullabies of the Maoris to the harp accompaniment of the Welsh bardic tradition. To see something of the relationship between music and storytelling, one only has to watch a film and listen to how the music and story interweave, or observe how music in theatre performances is used to enhance mood, or facilitate transitions. Although there are certain religious cultures that discourage the making of music, it seemingly remains a universal impulse, and Gardner (2006) suggests that musical intelligence is a specific function of the human brain.

If this is the case, and we also accept that storytelling is the most fundamental way in which people represent themselves to each other, then it is not unreasonable to suggest that music and the oral telling of story have a close affinity. The musicality of a telling is a significant ingredient in the poetic nature of the told story. In expressive storytelling, both the rhythm inherent in the way that words are combined and the ability to phrase and create cadences heighten the meaning of story for both listener and teller. Further, this musicality also extends to the para-linguistic elements of pitch and tone of voice, and the expressivity of the body, evoking mood, creating tension and bringing characters to life.

In this section, we look at two ways of integrating music and storytelling. In the first, we use Prokofiev's 'musical tale for children', *Peter and the Wolf*, as a stimulus to generate story. In the second part, music making is brought into the storytelling itself.

Music as a stimulus to storytelling

Peter and the Wolf

When children listen to music, it can generate vivid mental images and evoke deep emotions, reactions that can be naturally incorporated into story. Short pieces of music, or extracts of longer pieces, can be used in the classroom as part of a dialogic approach to storytelling by encouraging children to free-associate ideas with the music. The ideas that come from the group tale can form a narrative episode, which then can be expanded by placing it within the given basic story structure (abstract – problem – events leading to crisis – resolution – coda). The method therefore is similar to that suggested in Chapter 11, and in particular the worked example, *And When Did You Last See Your Father?*

It is also possible, however, to work with longer works, and *Peter and the Wolf* provides a ready-made narrative musical resource for storytelling. Written in 1936, it was scored for orchestra and narrator, and there are many recordings in which the narration is voiced by famous actors. There are, however, a few recordings available without the recorded narration, allowing the teacher to lead the children in shared storytelling [at the time of writing, these versions included those by the St Petersburg Radio and TV Orchestra conducted by Stanislav Gorkovenko (1994) and the London Philharmonic Orchestra conducted by Stephen Simon (2007)]. By constructing their own version of the narrative, rather than listening to a story, the children become involved in interpreting the music for themselves. Although Mills (2009) argues that we cannot know what children will hear in music, and should not assume that sounds create the same images for them as for us, in *Peter and the Wolf* the imagery created is held within a predetermined narrative structure.

While this approach is perhaps far from free-association, it does engage children as active and responsive listeners. In the process of storytelling, the children are entering into an emotional relationship with the music, based around the 'as if-ness' of the score in which events are played out by the orchestra. Sara Liptai suggests that children possess 'high levels of unconscious, unacknowledged visual and aural literacy' (2004: 133) and that talk around music should allow children to explore the aesthetics of the art form and not simply rehearse technical language. In this activity, although the language is bound by the grammar of story and character, children have the opportunity to express opinions and make creative links, as well as to use specific musical terminology.

Step 1 – Introducing the story of *Peter and the Wolf*

The activity is introduced as a story that the group will tell together. The story *Peter and the Wolf* isn't written down in a book, but is played by an orchestra.

List the characters in the story:

- Peter, a Russian boy, who likes playing in the meadow;
- Peter's grandfather, who is often grumpy;
- bird;
- duck;
- cat;
- wolf;
- hunters.

Discuss the kind of music/sounds that would suitably accompany these characters – it is worth noting that grandfather is grumpy, and the hunters are characterised by the firing of their guns. Make a note of suggested descriptive phrases on the board so that these can be incorporated into the storytelling. This discussion can incorporate specific musical terms and references:

volume	quiet (*piano*)	↔	loud (*forte*)
pitch	high	↔	low
speed	slow (*adagio*)	↔	fast (*allegro*)
articulation	separate, detached notes (*staccato*)	↔	smooth, connected notes (*legato*)
rhythm	even beats (- - - -)	↔	uneven beats (- — - -)

Although these terms may inform the musical discussion and generate associated descriptions, few of them will be incorporated within the storytelling itself.

This discussion leads children to ascribe sounds to attributes and behaviours that do not necessarily have a sound component (such as the waddling of a duck), and the resulting phrase bank provides a linguistic scaffold for the storytelling that follows. Although there will be ideas that cannot be used in the first instance because they do not match with Prokofiev's musical characterisations, they still help to frame the discussion around the language of story.

■ Peter (start the discussion with the sounds the children hear from each other playing at break times): music to suggest laughing, shouting, the sound of his feet when skipping, running or walking. Peter is playful, happy . . .

■ Duck: sounds to suggest quacking, waddling and splashing in water . . .

Step 2 – Telling the story of *Peter and the Wolf*

In this section, the story is told through a combination of the music, narration based on the given structure, and dialogue with the children. It is this dialogue that puts linguistic flesh on the narrative bones.

Each of the characters in the story is represented by a different instrument (or set of instruments) in the orchestra. As a visual aid, a set of cards could be prepared with pictures and names of the different musical instruments used to represent the characters:

■ strings (Peter);

■ flute (bird);

■ oboe (duck);

■ clarinet (cat);

■ bassoon (grandfather);

■ French horns (wolf);

■ kettle drums (hunters' guns).

It needs to be made clear, however, that these instruments are how Prokofiev has chosen to represent the characters. The children's ideas from Step 1 are as valid, but the composer of the piece may have made different choices.

The structure of *Peter and Wolf* is very simple, and is shown in Figure 13.1.

In the original piece, the narrative precedes each section of music. For this story-telling, the teacher provides a short introduction to each section before playing it;

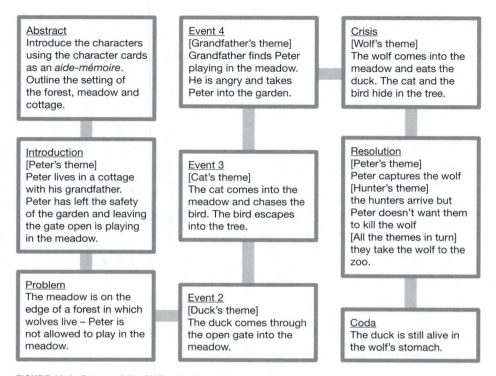

FIGURE 13.1 *Peter and the Wolf* – storyboard

whenever it feels right to expand the narrative, the music is paused. During these breaks, the teacher engages the children with the story, using the music as the stimulus (the phrase bank developed in Step 1 is a resource here). Care should be taken, however, not to pause the music mid-phrase; the music has a trajectory and, although it is interrupted, it should not be broken up so that it fails to make sense.

The story, and corresponding musical cues, are outlined in Table 13.1. The prompt questions are provided as a guide, but the aim is to construct a story rather than to generate one-word responses to the music. The questioning should therefore be shaped by dialogue. For example, if a child responds to the bird's flying into the meadow with 'the bird danced in the air around Peter's head', the following question should use this information, and seek to develop it: 'As the bird danced in the air around Peter's head, she said . . .'. In this way, children's responses are heard, valued and integrated into the narrative (see Chapter 5).

It should be noted that, although each character is defined by a particular instrument, children may not always be able to discern the differences between them. In particular, attention needs to be drawn to the different sounds made by the oboe (duck) and clarinet (cat). Perhaps sacrificing something of the flow of the music, the piece can be paused at critical points to highlight these distinctions (the prompt cards would be a helpful resource in this), remembering to respect the musical phrasing where possible (Table 13.1).

TABLE 13.1 *Peter and the Wolf*

STORY	MUSICAL CUE	SUGGESTED QUESTIONS
Once, long ago, there was a boy called Peter who lived with his grandfather in a cottage. Peter is allowed to play in the cottage's garden – but only when the strong garden gate is shut. For on the other side of the gate is a meadow, and on the edge of the meadow there is a forest, and in the forest there is a large wolf who is always hungry.	Peter's theme on the strings	What do you think Peter is doing in the meadow (dancing? skipping? playing?)? What do you think the garden looks like?
But one day, Peter is in the meadow	Bird's theme on the flute Peter's theme and the bird intertwine	Which character do you think this is? Where is she? What do you think she is saying? What do you think Peter and the bird are saying to each other?
In the meadow there is a pond. Someone can see the water . . .	The duck's oboe theme The duck's theme intertwines with that of the bird	Who do you think is going to the water, and why? What do you think the duck and the bird are arguing about? Where is the bird when she is arguing with the duck? How can we describe the bird and the duck?
But then Peter sees someone coming into the meadow – someone who has seen the bird, but the bird is arguing with the duck and she doesn't see the . . .	The cat's theme on the clarinet	Who doesn't she see? What do cats do? Wash their ears? Purr? What is she doing now? If she doesn't want the bird to see her, what will she be doing? Can you describe the cat jumping at the bird?
Then someone comes out of the cottage . . .	Grandfather's theme on the bassoon	Who is it? How does grandfather sound? Is he happy? Sad? Angry? How would you describe his voice?
Actually, he is angry because Peter is playing in the meadow not the garden – the meadow is dangerous because wolves live in the forest. Peter is taken back into the garden by his grandfather		If the meadow is a dangerous place to play, where do you think his grandfather wants Peter to be?

Narration	Theme	Questions
	The wolf's theme	Who is coming out of the forest? How do you think the wolf is moving?
The cat quickly scampers up the tree …	The cat's theme	
But the duck can't climb up a tree …	Duck's theme	What do you think the wolf is going to do? What do you think happens to the duck?
The cat and the bird are safely in the tree …	The themes of the wolf, bird and cat	What are the cat and the bird saying? Do you think they like being in the tree together?
Peter watches everything from the garden – he takes a rope, climbs onto the garden wall, and from the wall onto a branch of the tree ….	Peter's theme	
Peter sends the bird down to fly around the wolf's head …	Peter's and bird's theme intertwined	
	Wolf's theme and then bird's	What does the wolf think about the bird?
Peter makes a loop with the rope and …	Descending strings	What does he do with the rope? What do you think the wolf is trying to do?
Out of the forest comes a group of …	Hunters' theme with drums	Can you see them hunting the wolf with their guns? How do you think they are moving?
But Peter doesn't let the hunters kill the wolf. He wants to take the wolf somewhere safe ….	Instruments together / Each character's theme in turn	Where could they take the wolf? Peter and the hunters are taking the wolf to the zoo in a long procession – see if you can hear the different characters: Peter – hunters – wolf – hunters – grandfather and cat – bird – and …
If you listen carefully, you can hear the duck still alive inside the wolf's belly …	Duck's theme	
And that is the story of 'Peter and the Wolf', and that is how we have told it.	Flourish	Now, how do you think they can rescue the duck?

Step 3: Listening to the recording uninterrupted

Rather than listen to the whole of the piece again in the session, a recording (either with or without the original scored narration) could be made available to children to listen to as they wish.

Step 4: Plenary

In the plenary section, the discussion provides the opportunity to articulate the connections the children have made between the narrative and the qualities of the music. This will draw on:

- the choice of instruments to represent the characters;
- the way the music suggests different moods and actions (Peter's theme appears at the beginning to suggest a carefree boy, but is repeated in more sombre tones when Peter is trapping the wolf), and the similarities and differences between their own ideas and those of Prokofiev;
- how the rhythm of language can suggest different moods (reflecting the stimulus of the music), e.g. the style of narration when describing Peter playing can be compared with that associated with the wolf's entrance.

Children's aural literacy needs to be acknowledged as part of this process (Liptai, 2004). They bring experiences of many different forms of music to the classroom, and each child will have their own musical preferences. On this basis, children should be allowed to say when they don't see the things that Prokofiev intended them to see, and encouraged to make their own individual responses as they explore the qualities of music.

Integrating music in storytelling

Although music (such as *Peter and the Wolf* and traditional ballads) can be a vehicle for carrying narrative, or a stimulus for creating tales, music can also be included as an effective means of enhancing classroom storytelling. Integrated into a storytelling performance, music can add emotional emphasis and opportunities for participation, as well as providing cultural references. But in the context of storytelling as a social and linguistically flexible act, music-making does need to be a natural part of the telling and not simply an interlude – it continues to hold the participants in the imagined world, rather than providing a break from it.

In 2007, composer Howard Goodall was appointed as the National Ambassador for Singing; he wrote that, 'Singing makes us feel better about ourselves, enhances our self-esteem and sense of well-being, it allows us to work collaboratively within groups in a non-competitive, highly supportive environment' (2007). As a common practice in primary schools, singing provides an effective means of creating group cohesion and a common sense of purpose. This commonality of experience may be rooted in the very properties of the human voice, according to acoustics expert Jenny Zarek.

She has suggested that the human voice (perhaps unsurprisingly) has a natural resonance with, and creates sympathetic vibrations in, the body (cited by Daniel, 2008). When people sing together this effect is magnified, so that if singing is incorporated into group storytelling, the experience is not just aesthetic, but corporeal: the storytelling being felt through the body.

Songs, as a part of story, need to be short and memorable. A simple phrase can be repeated through the storytelling, or can develop through the narrative. In the former, the music serves to punctuate or enhance moments of the tale. In the latter, the developing song adds to the narrative, commenting on it or providing fresh information.

In 'The Well o' the World's End' (a Scottish variation of 'The Frog Prince'), I have used a simple folk refrain to develop the narrative. As the girl encounters the frog in a series of events, he sings to her; each time his song moves the story on:

Oh, where are you going, my hinny, my love?
Oh, where are you going my lady?
Oh, why do you weep, my hinny, my love . . .
Oh, open the door, my hinny, my love . . .
Oh, give me some milk, my hinny, my love . . .
Oh, chop off my head, my hinny my love . . .

This version of the story is somewhat more visceral than its French counterpart. The frog is transformed not by a kiss, but by having his head struck from his body. The sense of surprise at this unexpected turn in the narrative is enhanced by the instruction to behead coming in what (until this point) has simply been a charming folk ditty. The tune for this refrain is given in Figure 13.2.

In contrast to song as a means of developing the narrative, music that does not add new information can be used to indicate the passing of time, or a change of direction. 'The Snake Chief', the Xhosa version of 'Beauty and the Beast' (first written down in 1882 by George McCall Theal) has a strong sequential narrative that follows the contrasting fates of two sisters. In the first part, the older of the sisters follows a path through the forest to find the chief who will be her husband. Leaving her village without ceremony, and showing contempt for those she meets along the path, this sister scorns the traditions of her people and pays the price: the chief is a monstrous snake, and when she fails to show him due respect, she is eaten. In the second sequence, the younger sister respects both tradition and her elders, and is rewarded with a happy ending – the snake is transformed into a handsome chief, and they are married (see Figure 13.4).

Figure 13.3 shows a simple refrain, 'Hamba kahle', which means 'farewell' in Xhosa. I have used this chant to punctuate the storytelling and emphasise the mood at points

FIGURE 13.2 'The Well o' the World's End' – the frog's song

Ham-ba   Ham-ba   Ham-ba   Kah- le

FIGURE 13.3 'The Snake Chief' – chant

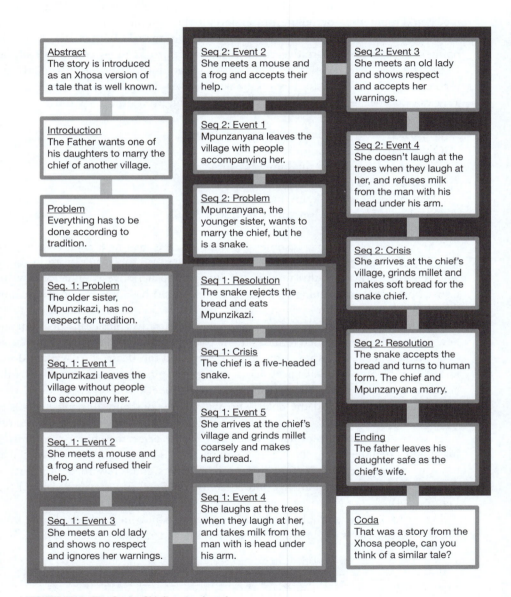

Abstract
The story is introduced as an Xhosa version of a tale that is well known.

Introduction
The Father wants one of his daughters to marry the chief of another village.

Problem
Everything has to be done according to tradition.

Seq. 1: Problem
The older sister, Mpunzikazi, has no respect for tradition.

Seq. 1: Event 1
Mpunzikazi leaves the village without people to accompany her.

Seq. 1: Event 2
She meets a mouse and a frog and refused their help.

Seq. 1: Event 3
She meets an old lady and shows no respect and ignores her warnings.

Seq 2: Event 2
She meets a mouse and a frog and accepts their help.

Seq 2: Event 1
Mpunzanyana leaves the village with people accompanying her.

Seq 2: Problem
Mpunzanyana, the younger sister, wants to marry the chief, but he is a snake.

Seq 1: Resolution
The snake rejects the bread and eats Mpunzikazi.

Seq 1: Crisis
The chief is a five-headed snake.

Seq 1: Event 5
She arrives at the chief's village and grinds millet coarsely and makes hard bread.

Seq 1: Event 4
She laughs at the trees when they laugh at her, and takes milk from the man with is head under his arm.

Seq 2: Event 3
She meets an old lady and shows respect and accepts her warnings.

Seq 2: Event 4
She doesn't laugh at the trees when they laugh at her, and refuses milk from the man with his head under his arm.

Seq 2: Crisis
She arrives at the chief's village, grinds millet and makes soft bread for the snake chief.

Seq 2: Resolution
The snake accepts the bread and turns to human form. The chief and Mpunzanyana marry.

Ending
The father leaves his daughter safe as the chief's wife.

Coda
That was a story from the Xhosa people, can you think of a similar tale?

FIGURE 13.4 'The Snake Chief' – storyboard

at which the narrative turns. When the older daughter leaves her village, refusing any ceremony to mark her going, the chant is what she hears as she goes into the forest. As she makes her way, treating the forest's inhabitants with contempt, the chant becomes quieter between each event as she gets further and further from home. When the younger sister travels through the forest (this time with accompanying singers and dancers to mark her betrothal), the chant is lively and rousing. At the end of the story, the new chief's wife listens to the chant fade as her father and friends return to their village.

The musical setting is a fragment of a Xhosa wedding song, and helps to reinforce the cultural origins of the story. The simple two-word refrain can be ascribed a variety of subtextual meanings (sadness, fear, rejoicing) through musical expression. To develop the children's competence in musical performance, the chant can be sung with varying expression, and can also be accompanied with percussion instruments – the children experimenting with different sounds to express the story's changing moods.

In both the above examples, the musical interludes are short enough for children to learn and develop for themselves. As part of this process, children should be exposed to related music, developing their own musical vocabulary that they can use in their own compositions. Mills (2009) sees composition as an essential element in children's musical education, and by relating the creation of music to story, it is given both a ready stimulus and a meaningful context.

Summary

Storytelling provides children with a context in which to explore a variety of musical forms. Without diminishing the value of studying music for its own sake, contextualising music in narrative provides a purpose for musical expression. This purpose provides a measure against which children are able to make their own judgements about the music. They can consider how a composer has tried to convey characters and emotional states in sound, and compare the images that the music conveys to them with those the composer intended.

In addition, children can learn to create and perform music that is integral to story, and to interpret narrative through their own music-making. Storytelling, then, can provide a context in which not only is music given meaning, but also meaning is drawn from music.

1 Introduction: storytelling as the social art of language

1. www.education.gov.uk/schools/teachingandlearning/pedagogy/nationalstrategies (please note that, at the time of publication, many of the materials from the National Strategies are in the process of being archived, but the archive website is in the process of development).

2 Building the framework: narrative structure and meta-narrative

1. 'Little Red Riding Hood' is available in many collections of the Grimms' fairy tales. The only complete collection of these that is currently in print is Grimm, J. and Grimm W. (1812), trans. Zipes, J. *The Complete Fairy Tales* (3rd edn, 2002). London: Vintage.
2. In fact, Charles Perrault's 1697 version of 'Little Red Riding Hood' is intended as a cautionary tale (including the instructional verse at the end):

> *On voit ici que de jeunes enfants,*
> *Surtout de jeunes filles*
> *Belles, bien faites, et gentilles,*
> *Font très mal d'écouter toute sorte de gens,*
> *Et que ce n'est pas chose étrange,*
> *S'il en est tant que le Loup mange.*
> *Je dis le Loup, car tous les Loups*
> *Ne sont pas de la même sorte ;*
> *Il en est d'une humeur accorte,*
> *Sans bruit, sans fiel et sans courroux,*
> *Qui privés, complaisants et doux,*
> *Suivent les jeunes Demoiselles*
> *Jusque dans les maisons, jusque dans les ruelles ;*
> *Mais hélas ! qui ne sait que ces Loups doucereux,*
> *De tous les Loups sont les plus dangereux.*

(http://chaperon.rouge.online.fr/perraultfr.htm)

This has been rendered into modern form by Neil Philip and Nicoletta Simborowski:

> Young children, as we clearly see,
> Pretty girls, especially,
> Innocent of all life's dangers,
> Shouldn't stop and chat with strangers.
> If this simple advice beats them,
> It's no surprise if a wolf eats them.

And this warning take, I beg:
Not every wolf runs on four legs.
The smooth tongue of a smooth skinned creature
May mask a rough and wolfish nature.
These quiet types, for all their charm,
Can be the cause of the worse harm.

(Philip and Simborowski, 1993: 34)

In this version, the absence of the huntsman – of a helper – means that the story is unresolved and falls into what Marie L. Shedlock (1915) referred to as the category of 'stories which appeal to fear or priggishness'.

4 Forging the tale anew: adapting the story for classroom telling

1. The 2005 animated film *Hoodwinked*, directed by Cory Edwards, plays with this idea and replays the same series events several times but from the perspectives of the different characters – we learn that the grandmother, far from being a sweet, helpless old lady, enjoys extreme sports and resents her granddaughter's patronising attitude to her age.
2. Thomas Bowdler (1754–1825) published an expurgated edition of Shakespeare in which, among other 'improvements', King Lear is reunited with his daughter Cordelia, and they go on to live happily at the end of the play.
3. The article that enables Cinderella's transformation from put-upon servant to princess varies (along with her name) from culture to culture: the glass shoe in France becomes the fur shoe in Eastern Europe, and the golden shoe in China. In some traditions the transformational object is a hat, and in others a ring; in Egypt, the girl's sandal is carried to Pharaoh by the gods.
4. By contrast with Aesop's tale, in which the tortoise overtakes the sleeping hare, versions found in the Netherlands and South Africa (in a Xhosa story) are closer to the English tale, with the tortoise's family arranging themselves along the race track. The tortoise pulls the same trick as he races the deer in Brazil, and the same method is employed by Siput the snail when he beats the bird in the Malaysian version of the race.

6 Words, words, words: storytelling, language and literacy

1. The application of storytelling to the teaching of SSP in this section is based on a Leading Partners in Literacy project, originally developed over three years (starting in 2008) at Kingston University, funded by the Training and Development Agency for Schools, and mirrored in 2010 by a joint project between London Metropolitan University and London Diocesan Board for Schools: School Centred Initial Teacher Training. While I provided university students and teachers from partnered schools with targeted training in storytelling as a pedagogic device, the project was initiated and managed by Pam Hodson at Kingston, and I am indebted to her for establishing the framework for the project and recognising the social potential for using storytelling in the context of SSP.
2. *Letters and Sounds*: www.education.gov.uk/publications/standard/publicationdetail/page1/DFES-00281-2007; *Read Write Inc.*: www.oup.com/oxed/primary/rwi/

7 Stories of pipers and tales of tall ships: history and geography through storytelling

1. Today, little remains of Newtown, but the town hall was restored in the early twentieth century and (at the time of writing) images can be found on the local history website at www.shalfleet.net/newtown
2. *A Point of View*, BBC Radio 4, 19 November 2010, www.bbc.co.uk/news/magazine-11743600

9 Possibility thinking: storytelling, science and mathematics

1. Interview, *The Forum*, BBC World Service, 22 August 2010.

11 Storytelling and the visual arts

1. The hierarchy of thinking skills is drawn from the revised version of Bloom's taxonomy suggested by Anderson and Krathwohl (2001), which moves from the low-level thinking involved in remembering to applying, analysing, evaluating and creating.

12 Storytelling, drama and dance: living the narrative

1. Cherie B. Stihler (2003) has written an alternative version, *The Giant Cabbage: An Alaska Folktale* (illustrated by Jeremiah Trammell), in which the farmer is a moose and the helpers are species native to North America.

Bibliography

Aesop (1964) *Fables of Aesop*, 2nd edn, trans. S.A. Handford. London: Penguin.

Alexander, R. (2008) *Towards Dialogic Teaching: Rethinking Classroom Talk*, 4th edn (first published 2004). Thirsk: Dialogos.

Alexander, R. (ed.) (2010) *Children, Their World, Their Education: Final Report and Recommendations of the Cambridge Primary Review*. London: Routledge.

Anderson, L.W. and Krathwohl, D.R. (2001) *A Taxonomy for Learning, Teaching and Assessing: A Revision of Bloom's Taxonomy of Educational Objectives*. New York: Longman.

Arnott, K. (1962) *African Myths and Legends*. Oxford, UK: Oxford University Press.

Barbe-Gall, F. (2005) *How to Talk to Children about Art*, trans. P. Dunn. London: Frances Lincoln.

Barrs, M. and Thomas, A. (eds) (1993) *The Reading Book*. London: Heinemann.

Bearne, E. (ed.) (1998) *The Use of Language across the Primary Curriculum*. London: Routledge.

Berry, C. (1989) *Voice and the Actor*. London: Virgin Books.

Bettelheim, B. (1976) *The Uses of Enchantment: The Meaning and Importance of Fairy Tales*. London: Penguin.

Blumenthal, E. (2005) *Puppetry and Puppets: An Illustrated World Survey*. London: Thames & Hudson.

Bolton, G. (1998) *Acting in Classroom Drama: A Critical Analysis*. Portland, ME: Calendar Island.

Booker, C. (2004) *The Seven Basic Plots: Why We Tell Stories*. London: Continuum.

Briggs, K. (1977) *British Folk-Tales and Legend*. London: Routledge.

Britton-Newell, L. (2007) 'What is Craft?'. London: Victoria and Albert Museum. www.vam.ac.uk/collections/contemporary/crafts/what_is_craft/index.html

Brook, P. (1968) *The Empty Space*. London: Penguin.

Browning, R. (1842) *The Pied Piper of Hamelin*. (1983) London: Methuen Children's Books.

Bruner, J. (1986) *Actual Minds, Possible Worlds*. Cambridge, MA: Harvard University Press.

Bruner, J. (1990) *Acts of Meaning*. Cambridge, MA: Harvard University Press.

Bruner, J. (2002) *Making Stories, Law, Literature, Life*. Cambridge, MA: Harvard University Press.

Butcher, S.E. (2006) 'Narrative as a teaching strategy', *Journal of Correctional Education*, 57(3): 195–208.

Campbell, J. (1949) *The Hero with a Thousand Faces* (1993 edn). London: Harper Collins.

Carter, D. (2002) *Shakespeare and Classic Works in the Classroom: Teaching pre-20th Century Literature at KS2 and KS3*. London: Routledge.

Corbett, P. (2008a) *Storyteller: Traditional Tales to Read, Tell and Write (Ages 7 to 9)*. Leamington Spa: Scholastic.

Corbett, P. (2008b) *Storytelling and Story-Making*. London: National Strategies/Department for Education and Skills.

Cortazzi, M. and Jin, L. (2007) 'Narrative learning, EAL and cognitive development', *Early Child Development and Care*, 177(6/7): 645–660.

Crace, J. (2007) 'Jerome Bruner: The Lesson of the Story', *The Guardian*, 27 March. www.guardian.co.uk/education/2007/mar/27/academicexperts.highereducationprofile

Craft, A. (2001) 'Little c Creativity', in Craft, C., Jeffrey, B. and Leibling, M. (eds), *Creativity in Education*. London: Continuum.

Cuddon, J.A. (1998) *The Penguin Dictionary of Literary Terms and Literary Theory*, 4th edn, rev. C.E. Preston. London: Penguin.

Daniel, A.K. (2007) 'From folktales to algorithms: developing the teacher's role as principal storyteller in the classroom', *Early Child Development and Care*, 177(6/7): 735–750.

Daniel, A.K. (2008) 'A comparative study of the spatial semiotics of contemporary theatre and Church of England liturgy', PhD thesis, University of Surrey.

Daniel, A.K. (2011) 'Teachers and children: a classroom community of storytellers' in D. Jones and P. Hodson (eds), *Unlocking Speaking and Listening* (2nd edn). London: David Fulton.

Datta, M. (2000) *Bilinguality and Literacy: Principles and Practice*. London: Continuum.

David, T. (2007) 'What is Early Childhood for', in K. Goouch and A. Lambirth (eds), *Understanding Phonics and the Teaching of Reading: Critical Perspectives*. Maidenhead, UK: Open University Press.

Davidson, N. (1985) *Astronomy and the Imagination: A New Approach to Man's Experience of the Stars*. London: Routledge and Kegan Paul.

Davies, J. and Donoghue, A. (1998) 'Teaching reading skills and history at Key Stage 2: a complementary approach', in P. Hoodless (ed.), *History and English in the Primary School: Exploiting the Links*. London: Routledge.

Dawkins, R. (2006) *The God Delusion*. London: Black Swan.

DCSF (2007) *Primary Framework for Literacy and Mathematics*. London: Department for Children, Schools and Families.

DCSF (2008a) *Talk for Writing*. London: Department for Children, Schools and Families.

DCSF (2008b) *Early Years Foundation Stage (EYFS) Pack*. London: Department for Children, Schools and Families. www.education.gov.uk/publications/standard/publicationDetail/Page1/DCSF-00261-2008

De La Mare, W. (1927) *Tales Told Again*. London: Faber and Faber.

DfEE (1999) *The National Curriculum: Handbook for Primary Teachers in England*. London: Department for Education and Employment/QCA.

DfEE (2003) *Speaking, Listening, Learning: Working with Children in Key Stages 1 and 2*. London: Department for Education and Employment/QCA.

Eder, D. and Holyan, R. (2010) *Life Lessons Through Storytelling: Children's Exploration of Ethics*. Bloomington, IN: University of Indiana Press.

Egan, K. (1986) *Teaching as Story Telling*. Chicago, IL: University of Chicago Press.

Egan, K. (1992) *Imagination in Teaching and Learning*. London: Routledge.

Farmer, A. and Cooper, C. (1998) 'Storytelling in history', in P. Hoodless (ed.), *History and English in the Primary School: Exploiting the Links*. London: Routledge.

Fisher, R. (2006a) '"Stories are for thinking": creative ways to share reading', in R. Fisher and M. Williams (eds), *Unlocking Literacy*. London: David Fulton.

Fisher, R. (2006b) 'Talking to think: why children need philosophical discussion', in D. Jones and P. Hodson (eds), *Unlocking Speaking and Listening*. London: David Fulton.

Foerst, A. (2005) *God in the Machine: What Robots Teach us about Humanity and God*. New York: Plume.

Fox, C. (1993). *At the Very Edge of the Forest: The Influence of Literature on Storytelling by Children*. London: Cassell.

Freytag, G. (1863) *Technique of the Drama: An Exposition of Dramatic Composition and Art*, trans. E.J. MacEwan (1900 edn). Chicago, IL: Scott, Foresman and Co.

Gardner, H. (2006) *Multiple Intelligences: New Horizons*. New York: Basic Books.

Glassie, H. (ed.) (1985) *Irish Folktales*. New York: Pantheon.

Glorieux-Desouche, I. (2006) *How to Talk to Children about World Art* (trans. P. Dunn 2010). London: Frances Lincoln.

Goffman, E. (1959) *The Presentation of Self in Everyday Life*. New York: Doubleday Anchor.

Goodall, H. (2007) 'Why all of Britain's schools should be singing from the same hymn sheet', *The Independent*, 25 October. www.independent.co.uk/news/education/schools/howard-goodall-why-all-of-britains-schools-should-be-singing-from-the-same-hymn-sheet-397756.html

Goouch, K. and Lambirth, A. (eds) (2007) *Understanding Phonics and the Teaching of Reading: Critical Perspectives*. Maidenhead: Open University Press.

Grainger, T. (1997) *Traditional Storytelling in the Primary Classroom*. Leamington Spa, UK: Scholastic.

Grainger, T. (2001) 'Crick Crack Chin my story's in – stories and storytelling', in P. Goodwin (ed.), *The Articulate Classroom: Talking and Learning in the Primary Classroom*. London: David Fulton.

Greimas, A.J. and Courtes, J. (1979) *Semiotics and Language, An Analytical Dictionary* (trans. Crist, L., Patte, D., McMohan II, E., Phillips, G. and Rengstorf, M., 1982). Bloomington, IN: Indiana University Press.

Greene, E. and Del Negro, J.M. (2010) *Storytelling Art and Technique* (4th edn). Santa Barbara, CA: Libraries Unlimited.

Griffiths, N. (2001) *Storysacks*. Reading, UK: Reading and Language Information Centre.

Grimm, J. and Grimm, W. (1812) in D. Lake (trans. and ed., 1982) *Jacob and Wilhelm Grimm Selected Tales*. London: Penguin.

Grimm, J. and Grimm, W. (2007) (trans. Zipes, J.) *The Complete Fairy Tales*. London: Vintage.

Grugeon, E. (2005) 'Listening to children's talk: oral language on the playground and in the classroom', in E. Grugeon, L. Daws, C. Smith and L. Hubbard (eds), *Teaching Speaking and Listening in Primary School* (3rd edn). London: David Fulton.

Grugeon, E. and Gardner, P. (2000) *The Art of Storytelling for Teachers and Pupils*. London: David Fulton.

Gussin Paley, V. (1990) *The Boy Who Would Be A Helicopter: The Uses Of Storytelling In The Classroom*. Cambridge, MA: Harvard University Press.

Hall, E.T. (1966) *The Hidden Dimension*. Garden City, NY: Doubleday.

Hardy, B. (1978) 'Narrative as a primary act of mind', in M. Meek, A. Warlow and G. Barton (eds), *The Cool Web: The Pattern of Children's Reading*. New York: Atheneum.

Harrett, J. (2009) *Tell Me Another . . . Speaking, Listening and Learning through Storytelling* (2nd edn). Leicester: United Kingdom Literacy Association.

Haven, K. (2007) *Story Proof: The Science behind the Startling Power of Story*. London: Libraries Unlimited.

Hawkes, T. (2003) *Structuralism and Semiotics* (2nd edn). London: Routledge.

Hearne, B. (1993) *Oryx Multicultural Folktale Series: Beauties and Beasts*. Phoenix, AZ: Oryx Press.

Heathcote, D. and Bolton, G. (1995) *Drama for Learning: Dorothy Heathcote's Mantle of the Expert Approach to Education*. Portsmouth, NH: Heinemann.

Hendy, L. and Toon, L. (2001) *Supporting Drama and Imaginative Play in the Early Years*. Buckingham, UK: Open University Press.

bin Hitam, Z. (1995) *Folk Tales of Malaysia*. New Delhi: Learners Press.

Hitchens, P. (2010) 'The other L-word', *Vanity Fair*, 10 January. www.vanityfair.com/culture/features/2010/01/hitchens-like-201001

Hoffman, M. and Ray, J. (1998) *Sun, Moon and Stars*. London: Orion.

Homan, R. (2000) 'Don't let the murti get dirty: the uses and abuses of "artefacts"', *British Journal of Religious Education*, 23(1): 27–37.

Hoodless, P. (1998) 'Children's awareness of time', in P. Hoodless (ed.), *History and English in the Primary School: Exploiting the Links*. London: Routledge.

Howe, A. and Johnson, J. (1992) *Common Bonds: Storytelling in the Classroom*. London: Hodder & Stoughton/National Oracy Project.

Hughes, G. (2003). *Worship as Meaning*. Cambridge, UK: Cambridge University Press.

Hyvärinen, M. (2006) 'Towards a conceptual history of narrative', *Collegium: Studies across Disciplines in the Humanities and Social Sciences*, 1: 20–41. www.helsinki.fi/collegium/e series/volumes/volume_1/001_04_hyvarinen.pdf

Irish, T. (2007) *Stand Up for Shakespeare: Classroom Research*. Stratford, UK: Royal Shakespeare Company. www.rsc.org.uk/downloads/rsc_sufs_classroom_research_141210.pdf

Isbell, R., Sobol, J., Lindauer, L. and Lowrance, A. (2004) 'The effects of storytelling and story reading on the oral language complexity and story comprehension of young children', *Early Childhood Education*, 32(3): 157–163.

Jacobs, J. (1890) *English Fairy Tales*. London: Everyman's Library.

Jacobs, J. (1894) *More English Fairy Tales*. London: Everyman's Library.

James, G. (1912) *Japanese Fairy Tales*. London: Senate.

Jones, G. (2010) 'Picture this', *Drama*, 17(1): 2–7.

Kaplin, S. (2001) 'A puppet tree, a model for the field of puppet theatre', in John Bell (ed.), *Puppets, Masks and Performing Objects*. Cambridge, MA: New York University and Massachusetts Institute of Technology.

Kirk, G.S. (1974) *The Nature of the Greek Myths*. London: Penguin.

Laban, R. (1950) *The Mastery of Movement* (ed. Lisa Ullman, 4th edn, 1980). Plymouth, UK: Macdonald and Evans.

Labov, W. (1972) *Sociolinguistic Patterns*. Philadelphia, PA: University of Pennsylvania Press.

Lacey, R. (2006) *Great Tales from English History: The Battle of the Boyne to DNA*. London: Little, Brown.

Larson, J. and Marsh, J. (2005) *Making Literacy Real: Theories and Practices for Learning and Teaching*. London: Sage.

Lewis, R. (2006) 'Scaffolding learning: speaking, listening and EAL pupils', in D. Jones and P. Hodson (eds), *Unlocking Speaking and Listening*. London: Routledge.

Lipman, D. (1999) *Improving Your Storytelling*. Little Rock, AR: August House.

Liptai, S. (2004) 'Creativity in music and art', in R. Fisher and M. Williams (eds), *Unlocking Creativity*. London: David Fulton.

Livo, N. and Rietz, S. (1986) *Storytelling: Process and Practice*. Littleton, CO: Libraries Unlimited.

Lyle, S. (2000) 'Narrative understanding: developing a theoretical context for understanding how children make meaning in classroom settings', *Curriculum Studies*, 32(1): 45–63.

Mallett, M. (2002). *The Primary English Encyclopaedia: The Heart of the Curriculum*. London: David Fulton.

Martin, B. (1997) *Storytelling and Semiotics*. Dublin: Philomel.

Matthews, A. (1996) *How the World Began and Other Stories of Creation*. Hove, UK: Macdonald.

Mawle, A. (2010) 'Out of Art Into Literacy' (video transcript), www.nationalgallery.org.uk/server.php?show=conMediaFile.15491&showTranscript=1

McCall Theal, G. (1882) *Kaffir Folk-lore, or, A Selection from the Traditional Tales Current among the People Living on the Eastern Border of the Cape Colony with Copious Explanatory Notes*. London: W. Swan Sonnenschein.

McDonald, M. (1996) *Tales of the Constellations: The Myths and Legends of the Night Sky*. New York: Smithmark.

Mills, J. (2009) *Music in the Primary School* (3rd edn). Oxford, UK: Oxford University Press.

NACCCE (1999) *All Our Futures: Creativity, Culture and Education*. London: DfEE, National Advisory Committee on Creative and Cultural Education.

Newall, D. (2008) *Appreciating Art*. London: A & C Black.

Ofsted (2007) *History in the Balance: History in English Schools 2003–07*. London: Ofsted.

O'Neill, C. (1995) *Drama Worlds: A Framework for Process Drama*. London: Heinemann.

O'Neill, D.K., Pearce, M.J. and Pick, J.L. (2004) 'Preschool children's narratives and performance on the Peabody Individualized Achievement Test – Revised: Evidence of a relation between early narrative and later mathematical ability', *First Language*, 24(2): 149–183.

Pellowski, A. (1977) *The World of Storytelling*. New York: R.R. Bowker.

Perrault, C. (1697) *Little Red Riding Hood and other Classic Stories*, trans. N. Philip and N. Simborowski (1993 edn). London: Pavilion.

Philip, N. (ed.) (1992) *The Penguin Book of English Folktales*. London: Penguin.

Philip, N. (1997) *The Illustrated Book of Fairy Tales*. London: Dorling Kindersley.

Pollerman, S. (2001) *Stories, Stories Everywhere*. Oxford, UK: Bible Reading Fellowship.

Porter-Abbott, H. (2002) *The Cambridge Introduction to Narrative*. Cambridge: Cambridge University Press.

Potter, B. (1982) *The Complete Adventures of Peter Rabbit*. London: Penguin.

Propp, V. (1928) *Morphology of the Folktale*, trans. L. Scott, ed. Louis A. Wagner (2nd edn, 1968). Austin, TX: University of Texas Press.

Quinion, M. (2000) *Port Out, Starboard Home: The Fascinating Stories We Tell about the Words We Use*. London: Penguin.

Reed, A.W. (1998). *Aboriginal Fables and Legendary Tales*. Sydney: Reed New Holland.

Ricoeur, P. (1984) *Time and Narrative*. K. McLaughlin and D. Pellauer (trans.). Chicago, IL: University of Chicago Press.

Rosen, Betty (1990) *And None of it Was Nonsense*. London: Mary Glasgow.

Rosen, Betty (1991) *Shapers and Polishers*. London: Mary Glasgow.

Rosenberg, D. (1997) *Folklore, Myths and Legends: A World Perspective*. Lincolnwood, IL: NTC.

Rowcliffe, S. (2004) 'Storytelling in science', *School Science Review*, 86(314): 121–126.

Rowlands, S., Graham, T. and Berry, J. (2005) 'The Vygotskian perspective and the radical versus the social constructivism debate'. www.bsrlm.org.uk/IPs/ip16-3/BSRLM-IP-16-3-9.pdf

Rushdie, S. (1990) *Haroun and the Sea of Stories*. London: Penguin.

Ryan, P. (1997) *Word in Action*. Londonderry: Verbal Arts Centre.

Ryokai, K., Vaucelle, C. and Cassell, J. (2003) 'Virtual peers as partners in storytelling and literacy learning', *Journal of Computer Assisted Learning*, 19: 195–208.

Schama, S. (2000) *A History of Britain: At the Edge of the World? 3000 BC–AD 1603*. London: BBC.

Schank, R.C. (1990) *Tell me a Story: Narrative and Intelligence*. Evanston, IL: Northwestern University Press.

Schechner, R. (1985) *Between Theatre and Anthropology*. Philadelphia, PA: University of Pennsylvania.

Schechner, R. (1990) 'Magnitudes of performance', in R. Schechner and W. Appel (eds), *By Means of Performance: Intercultural Studies of Theatre and Ritual*. Cambridge, UK: Cambridge University Press.

Schechner, R. (2003) *The Future of Ritual: Writings on Culture and Performance*. London: Routledge.

Schechner, R. (2006) *Performance Studies: An Introduction* (2nd edn). London: Routledge.

Scherba de Valenzuela, J. (undated) 'Definitions of "decontextualised" and "contextualised" language', University of New Mexico website, www.unm.edu/~devalenz/handouts/decontext2.html

Schiro, M.S. with Lawson, D. (2004). *Oral Storytelling and Teaching Mathematics: Pedagogical and Multicultural Perspectives*. London: Sage.

Schleifer, R. (1987) *A.J. Greimas and the Nature of Meaning: Linguistics, Semiotics and Discourse Theory*. Lincoln, NE: University of Nebraska Press.

Seki, K. (1963) *Folktales of Japan*, trans. R.J. Adams. Chicago, IL: University of Chicago Press.

Shakespeare, W. (1951) *Macbeth* (The Arden Shakespeare). London: Methuen.

Shakespeare, W. (1992) *Macbeth*, in *Shakespeare: The Animated Tales*, ed. L. Garfield. London: Heinemann.

Shedlock, M.L. (1915) *The Art of the Storyteller* (2008 edn), Forgotten Books. www:forgottenbooks.org

Sherman, J. (2003) *Mythology for Storytellers: Themes and Tales from Around the World*. Armonk, NY: Sharpe Reference.

Sierra, J. (1992) *The Oryx Multicultural Series: Cinderella*. Westport, CT: Oryx Press.

Smith, P. (1992) *Japanese Fairy Tales*. New York: Dover.

Smith, P.K., Cowie, H. and Blades, M. (2003) *Understanding Children's Development* (4th edn). Oxford, UK: Blackwell.

Solity, J. (2003) 'Teaching phonics in context: a critique of the National Literacy Strategy', paper presented to DfES Seminar, *Teaching Phonics in the National Literacy Strategy*, 17 March 2003, http://core.roehampton.ac.uk/digital/general/critique.pdf.

Stern, A. (1996) *Tales from Many Lands: An Anthology of Multicultural Folk Literature*. Lincolnwood, IL: National Textbook Company.

Stihler, C.B. (2003) *The Giant Cabbage: An Alaska Folktale*. Seattle: Sasquatch Books.

Swann Jones, S. (2002) *The Fairy Tale*. London: Routledge.

Sylvester, R. and Thomson, A. (2010) 'It's not about class, it's about the classroom, says Gove', *The Times*, 6 March. www.timesonline.co.uk/tol/news/politics/article7052100.ece

Tan, S. (2007) *The Arrival*. London: Hodder Children's Books.

Tatar, M. (1992) *Off With Their Heads! Fairy Tales and the Culture of Childhood*. Princeton, NJ: Princeton University Press.

Tatar, M. (ed.) (1999) *The Classic Fairy Tale*. New York: W.W. Norton.

Tatar, M. (1987) *The Hard Facts of the Grimm's Fairy Tales* (2nd edn, 2003). Princeton, NJ: Princeton University Press.

Tatar, M. (ed.) (2004) *The Annotated Fairy Tales*. New York: W.W. Norton.

Tatar, M. (ed.) (2008a) *The Annotated Hans Christian Andersen*. New York: W.W. Norton.

Tatar, M. (ed.) (2008b) *The Annotated Brothers Grimm*. New York: W.W. Norton.

Thompson, S. (1946) *The Folktale*. Berkeley, CA: University of California Press.

Tiemensma, L. (2010) 'Books are windows, books are mirrors: multicultural collections for children and young adults opening new worlds', address to the World Library and Information Congress, 76th IFLA General Conference and Assembly, Gothenburg, Sweden. www.ifla.org/files/hq/papers/ifla76/147–tiemensma-en.pdf

Toolan, M. (2001) *Narrative: A Critical Linguistic Introduction* (2nd edn). London: Routledge.

Turner, V. (1982) *From Ritual to Theatre: The Human Seriousness of Play*. New York: PAJ Publications.

Turner-Bisset, R. (2005) *Creative Teaching: History in the Primary Classroom*. London: David Fulton.

Vygotsky, L. (1978) *Mind and Society*. Cambridge, MA: Harvard University Press.

Westwood, J. and Simpson, J. (2005) *The Lore of the Land: A Guide to England's Legends, From Spring-Heeled Jack to the Witches of Warboys*. London: Penguin.

Wilde, O. (1891) *The Picture of Dorian Gray* (repr. 1988). London: Penguin Classics.

Winnicott, D.W. (1971) *Playing and Reality*. London: Routledge.

Winston, J. (1998) *Drama, Narrative and Moral Education*. Abingdon, UK: Routledge Falmer.

Wood, D. (1998) *How Children Think and Learn*. Oxford, UK: Blackwell.

Wyse, D. and Jones, R. (2008) *Teaching English, Language and Literacy*. London: Routledge.

Zipes, J. (1994) *Fairy Tale as Myth: Myth as Fairy Tale*. Lexington, KY: University Press of Kentucky.

Zipes, J. (1995) *Creative Storytelling*. London: Routledge.

Zipes, J. (1997) *Happily Ever After: Fairy Tales, Children and the Culture Industry*. London: Routledge.

Zipes, J. (1999) *When Dreams Came True: Classical Fairy Tales and their Tradition*. London: Routledge.

Zipes, J. (2004) *Speaking Out, Storytelling and Creative Drama for Children*. London: Routledge.

VIDEO RECORDINGS

Gussin Paley, V. (2001) *The Boy Who Could Tell Stories*, Armstrong, D. and Dawson, M. (dirs). Muncie, IN: Ball State University.

AUDIO RECORDINGS

Nyman, M. (1992) *The Essential Michael Nyman Band* on Argo Records.

Prokoviev, S. (1994) *Peter and the Wolf*, St Petersburg Radio and TV Orchestra conducted by Stanislav Gorkovenko on Sony Classical.

REFERENCED STORIES AND THEIR SOURCES

Chapter 2

'The Sage Duban', in Mahdi, M. (ed.) (1990) *The Arabian Nights*, trans. Husain Haddaway. New York: W.W. Norton.

'Little Red Riding Hood' or 'Little Red Cap', in Grimm, J. and Grimm, W. (2007) *Grimm: The Complete Fairy Tales*, trans. J. Zipes. London: Vintage, p. 125.

'Little Red Riding Hood', in Perrault, C. (1697) *Little Red Riding Hood and other Classic Stories*, trans. N. Philip and N. Simborowski (repr. 1993). London: Pavilion, pp. 30–34.

'The Fox and the Wild Goose' (Scotland), retold by John Francis Campbell, in Crossley-Holland, K. (ed.) (1985) *Folk-Tales of the British Isles*. London: Faber and Faber, p. 220.

The Tale of Peter Rabbit, Potter, B. (1902). London: Warne.

'The Oyster Bothers and the Shark', retold by Reed, A.W. in *Aboriginal Fables and Legendary Tales* (1998). Sydney: Reed New Holland, pp. 98–100.

'The Story of Brookland Bell Tower', in Westwood, J. and Simpson, J. (2005) *The Lore of the Land: A Guide to England's Legends, From Spring-Heeled Jack to the Witches of Warboys*. London: Penguin, p. 375.

Heracles, stories of, retold by Green, R.L. (1958) in *Tales of the Greek Heroes*. London: Penguin.

'Robin Hood of Sherwood Forest', retold by Bulfinch, T. (1858) *Bulfinch's Mythology: The Age of Chivalry*. New York: Macmillan.

'The Giant's Skull', in Hoffman, M. and Ray, J. (1998) *Sun, Moon and Stars*. London: Orion.

Chapter 3

'Mr Fox', in Jacobs, J. (1894) *English Fairy Tales* (1993 edn). London: Everyman's Library, p. 147.

'Bluebeard', in Perrault, C. (1697) *Little Red Riding Hood and other Classic Stories*, trans. N. Philip and N. Simborowski (repr. 1993). London: Pavilion, pp. 30–34.

'The Three Billy Goats Gruff', variations available at D.L. Ashliman's website hosted by the University of Pittsburgh, www.pitt.edu/~dash/type0122e.html

Chapter 4

The Tale of Troy, Green, R.L. (1958). London: Puffin.
'The Fisherman and his Wife' and 'The Hare and the Hedgehog', in Grimm, J. and Grimm, W. (2007) *Grimm: The Complete Fairy Tales*, trans. J. Zipes. London: Vintage, p. 89.
'Cinderella', variations can be found in Sierra, J. (1992) *The Oryx Multicultural Series: Cinderella*. Westport, CT: Oryx Press.
'Snow White', in Grimm, J. and Grimm, W. (2007) *Grimm: The Complete Fairy Tales*, trans. J. Zipes. London: Vintage, p. 237.
'Manypelts' or 'All Fur', in Grimm, J. and Grimm, W. (2007) *Grimm: The Complete Fairy Tales*, trans. J. Zipes. London: Vintage, p. 316.
'Little Red Riding Hood', in Zipes, J. (1995) *Creative Storytelling*. London: Routledge.
'The Hare and the Tortoise', in *Fables of Aesop*, trans. S.A. Handford (2nd edn, 1964). London: Penguin, p. 70.
'The Hare and the Hedgehog', in Grimm, J. and Grimm, W. (2007) *Grimm: The Complete Fairy Tales*, trans. J. Zipes. London: Vintage, p. 729.
'The Hare and the Hedgehog', retold by de la Mare, W. (1927) *Tales Told Again*. London: Faber and Faber, p. 9.
'Siput the Snail', retold by bin Hitam, Z. (1995) *Folk Tales of Malaysia*. New Delhi: Learners Press, pp. 57–60.
'The Tortoise Wins a Race' (Brazil), retold by Stern, A. (1996) *Tales from Many Lands: An Anthology of Multicultural Folk Literature*. Lincolnwood, IL: National Textbook Company, pp. 77–84.
'How the Hedgehog ran the Devil to Death', recounted by The Reverend T.H. Philpott to Ella Mary Leather (1912), in Philip, N. (ed.) (1992) *The Penguin Book of English Folktales*. London: Penguin, p. 395.

Chapter 5

'The Happy Prince', in Wilde, O. (1888) *The Happy Prince and Other Stories* (1962 edn). London: Puffin.
'How the Crab got a Hard Back', in Sherlock, P. (1966) *Oxford Myths and Legends: West Indian Folk-tales*. Oxford, UK: Oxford University Press, p. 86.

Chapter 6

'The Old Woman and her Pig', in Rackham, A. (ed.) (1994) *Mother Goose: Old Nursery Rhymes*. Ware, UK: Wordsworth Classics.

Chapter 7

'The Hare and the Tortoise', in *Fables of Aesop*, trans. S.A. Handford (2nd edn, 1964). London: Penguin, p. 70.
'How the Hedgehog ran the Devil to Death', recounted by The Reverend T.H. Philpott to Ella Mary Leather (1912), in Philip, N. (ed.) (1992) *The Penguin Book of English Folktales*. London: Penguin, p. 395.
'The Snake Chief', in Arnott, K. (1962) *African Myths and Legends*. Oxford, UK: Oxford University Press, pp. 186–194.
'Beauty and the Beast', variations can be found in Hearne, B. (1993) *Oryx Multicultural Folktale Series: Beauties and Beasts*, Phoenix, AZ: Oryx Press.
'The Pied Piper of Hamelin', in Crossley-Holland, K. (1998) *The Young Oxford Book of Folk-Tales*. Oxford, UK: Oxford University Press, p. 85.
'The Pied Piper' (of Newtown, Isle of Wight), in Jacobs, J. (1894) *English Fairy Tales* (repr. 1993). London: Everyman's Library, p. 225.
The Pied Piper of Hamelin, Browning, R. (1842; 1983 edn). London: Methuen Children's Books.

Chapter 8

'The Old Man and his Grandson', in Grimm, J. and Grimm, W. (2007) *Grimm: The Complete Fairy Tales*, trans. J. Zipes. London: Vintage, p. 353.

Chapter 9

'Orion', in McDonald, M. (1996) *Tales of the Constellations: The Myths and Legends of the Night Sky*. New York: Smithmark, pp. 109–113.

The Hebrew creation myth as recorded in the Book of Genesis, chapters 1 and 2.

'Amei Awi and Berung Une', a creation myth of the Dyak people of Borneo, in Matthews, A. (1996) *How the World Began and Other stories of Creation*. Hove, UK: Macdonald, pp. 48–51.

Haroun and the Sea of Stories, Salman Rushdie (1990). London: Penguin.

Chapter 11

'The Snake Chief', in Arnott, K. (1962) *African Myths and Legends*. Oxford, UK: Oxford University Press, pp. 186–194.

'Urashima Taro', in Seki, K. (1963) *Folktales of Japan*, trans. R.J. Adams. Chicago, IL: Chicago University Press.

Chapter 12

'The Gigantic Turnip', several picture-book versions are available [including that by Alexei Tolstoy with illustrations by Niamh Sharky (1999), Oxford, UK: Barefoot Books], and there are multilingual editions of the version by Henriette Barkow with illustrations by Richard Johnson (2001), London: Mantra Lingua.

The Arrival, by Shaun Tan (2007). London: Hodder Children's Books.

Chapter 13

'The Well o' the World's End', by Elizabeth Grierson, in G. Jarvie (ed.) (1997) *Scottish Folk and Fairy Tales*. London: Penguin.

'The Snake Chief' (originally found in McCall Theal, 1882), retold in Arnott, K. (1962) *African Myths and Legends*. Oxford, UK: Oxford University Press, pp. 186–194.

WEB SOURCES

Constellations of words: www.constellationsofwords.com

Primary Resources: www.primaryresources.co.uk/maths/probsfoot.htm

Aarne-Thompson Folktale Types – a guide by Scott Mellor: http://scandinavian.wisc.edu/mellor/taleballad/pdf_files/motif_types.pdf

Tate Gallery: www.tate.co.uk

Liverpool Walker Gallery: www.liverpoolmuseums.org.uk

Index